# THE *Sunset* GROUND BEEF COOK BOOK

**By the editors of Sunset Books and Sunset Magazine**

SECOND PRINTING JULY 1965
ALL RIGHTS RESERVED THROUGHOUT THE WORLD. COPYRIGHT © 1965 BY
LANE MAGAZINE & BOOK COMPANY, MENLO PARK, CALIFORNIA. LIBRARY
OF CONGRESS CATALOG CARD: 65-16752. TITLE NUMBER 245. LITHOGRAPHED
IN UNITED STATES OF AMERICA.

**LANE BOOKS · MENLO PARK, CALIF.**

*Giant open-faced hamburgers (recipe opposite) are built upon a base of split round French bread loaf. Tomato, cucumber half-slices top each individual serving.*

# BEEF PATTIES

## 29 ways to vary them

### Broiled Beef Patties with Quick Stroganoff Sauce

1 pound ground beef
1 teaspoon salt
¼ teaspoon pepper
1 package (¾ oz.) mushroom gravy mix
1 tablespoon instant toasted onion
½ teaspoon paprika
½ cup sour cream
3 English muffins, split, buttered, and toasted

Combine ground beef, salt, and pepper, and form into 6 patties. Prepare mushroom gravy according to directions on the package. Add toasted onion and paprika. Keep hot (but not boiling) while you broil the beef patties until done to your liking. Just before serving, blend sour cream into mushroom gravy. To serve, place a beef patty on each toasted English muffin half, and spoon sauce over. Makes 6 servings.

### Hamburger Supreme

Diced Brazil nuts are the unusual ingredient in these hamburgers.

1 pound ground beef
10 Brazil nuts, diced
1 teaspoon salt
¼ teaspoon pepper
1 tablespoon barbecue sauce or steak sauce
1 tablespoon catsup
1 slice white bread (minus crust), soaked in water and squeezed until just moist

Mix above ingredients and form into 6 medium-sized patties. Broil for 3 to 5 minutes on each side. Makes 6 servings.

### Hamburger Steak in the Round

Rich meat juices mingle with a mustard and chili-seasoned butter, then sink into the French bread as you grill these giant hamburgers over hot coals.

1 round loaf French bread
¼ pound soft butter
½ teaspoon prepared mustard
½ teaspoon chili powder
3 pounds ground chuck
2 teaspoons seasoned salt
½ cup finely chopped green onions with tops
2 tablespoons chili sauce
1 tablespoon soy sauce or Worcestershire
Thin cucumber and tomato half-slices

Cut French bread in half horizontally, and spread cut slices with seasoned barbecue butter made by blending the butter, mustard, and chili powder. Lightly mix together the ground chuck, seasoned salt, green onions, chili sauce, and soy sauce. Shape into 2 round patties each a little larger than the bread (the meat shrinks slightly when cooked). Place bread, crust side down, at back of grill (away from hottest coals) to heat slowly. Barbecue meat patties on one side until browned and partially done. Turn patties, and place bread, buttered side down, on top of them. Continue grilling patties until undersides are browned and meat is cooked to degree of doneness desired.

To serve, turn meat and bread onto serving platter with bread on bottom, meat on top. Garnish with alternating cucumber and tomato slices placed on top of meat patties, slightly overlapping slices in a row to mark each individual portion. Cut each round into 5 wedges to serve. Makes 10 servings.

# German Beef Patties *(see suggested menu below)* *

1½ pounds ground chuck
1½ cups grated raw carrot (about 2 carrots)
⅓ cup chopped onion
1½ teaspoons salt
¼ teaspoon pepper
2 tablespoons butter or margarine
1 can (10½ oz.) beef bouillon
¾ cup water
¼ cup lemon juice
8 gingersnaps, finely crushed
1 large package (12 oz.) wide egg noodles
2 tablespoons butter or margarine

Combine ground chuck, carrot, onion, salt, and pepper. Shape into 6 patties, about 1 inch thick. Melt 2 tablespoons butter in a frying pan, and brown meat patties on both sides (takes about 5 minutes). Combine bouillon, water, and lemon juice, and pour over patties. Sprinkle crushed gingersnaps over patties and liquid, stirring until sauce is smooth. Cover and simmer for 10 minutes.

Meanwhile, cook noodles according to directions on package. Drain, and add 2 tablespoons butter and toss lightly. Serve meat mixture over noodles. Makes 6 servings.

# * Quick Weekday Family Dinner

German Beef Patties *(see recipe above)*
Hot Buttered Noodles
Tossed Green Salad
Buttered Peas and Mushrooms
Hot Rolls
Top Crust Apple Pie

There are ways to make weekday family dinners as interesting as guest meals without going to extensive preparations. For example, these German Beef Patties in a sauerbraten-like sauce, served over wide egg noodles, take only about 30 minutes to prepare, yet have a rich flavor suggesting a much longer cooking time. You can make the dessert ahead and warm it in the oven before you serve it, if you wish. While the beef patties are simmering, cook the noodles and the frozen peas and mushrooms. Make or buy the hot rolls, and use your favorite version of tossed green salad.

## Top Crust Apple Pie

4 large cooking apples, pared and thinly sliced
½ cup granulated sugar
2 tablespoons lemon juice
2 tablespoons orange juice
½ cup brown sugar, firmly packed
1 cup flour
½ teaspoon cinnamon
½ cup (¼ pound) butter or margarine
Vanilla ice cream or whipped cream (optional)

Pour apples into a buttered 9-inch pie pan, and sprinkle with the granulated sugar, lemon juice, and orange juice. Combine brown sugar, flour, and cinnamon. Cut in butter until mixture is crumbly. Pat evenly over the top of apples. Bake in a hot oven (400°) for 30 minutes or until apples are tender. Cool and slice in wedges to serve. Top with small scoops of vanilla ice cream or whipped cream, if you wish. Makes 6 servings.

## Hamburger Orientale

East and West effect a meeting in his recipe for ground beef patties. They have a Japanese teriyaki flavor and a Scandinavian meat ball texture. Don't overcook; the rarer they are, the juicier they remain.

4 dried mushroom caps
Water
1 pound ground round
2 tablespoons soy sauce
1½ teaspoons ground ginger
Cayenne pepper
Monosodium glutamate
2 tablespoons olive oil

Soak dried mushroom caps in water for 30 minutes to 1 hour. Place ground round in a bowl, make a crater in the middle, pour in the soy sauce, and sprinkle with the ginger and a light sprinkling of cayenne pepper and monosodium glutamate. Drain mushrooms, cut into pieces about ¼ inch square, and place in crater.

Mix the meat with all the other ingredients by hand until all are well blended. Divide into 3 patties, each about ½ inch thick. Pour olive oil into a frying pan and place over medium heat; when hot, put patties in, cook until browned on both sides and done to taste. Makes 3 servings.

## Grilled Blue Cheese Patties

The flavor of these thick grilled hamburger patties is enriched by blue cheese, deviled ham, and a preliminary marinating in wine.

1 pound lean ground beef
1 small can (2 or 3 oz.) deviled ham
Pinch each salt and pepper
4 pieces blue cheese, each cut about 1¼ inches
    square and ½ inch thick
Red table wine

Combine ground beef, deviled ham, salt, and pepper. Divide into 4 portions, and mold each around a piece of cheese. Place in a bowl, cover with wine, and allow to marinate, covered, in the refrigerator for about 3 hours. Remove from wine marinade and grill over charcoal or broil until done to taste. Makes 4 servings.

## Beef Patties with Pineapple Sauce

Apple sauce goes inside the meat patties and a pineapple sauce on top.

1 pound ground beef
1 teaspoon salt
¼ teaspoon freshly ground pepper
1 cup thick apple sauce
2 tablespoons brown sugar
3 tablespoons cider vinegar
½ teaspoon dry mustard
1 small can (9 oz.) pineapple tidbits
Pinch of ground ginger

Mix together the ground beef, salt, pepper, and apple sauce, and shape into 6 patties. Place on a rack and broil for 5 minutes on each side, or until browned and as well done as you wish. Meanwhile, mix together the brown sugar, vinegar, mustard, 2 tablespoons of the pineapple syrup, and ginger. Heat, stirring until blended; then add the pineapple tidbits (drained) and heat thoroughly. Arrange patties on a hot platter and pour sauce over them. Makes 6 servings.

## Ground Beef Relish Patties

Here is one way to simplify serving of the "hamburger"—relishes are cooked inside the ground meat patty.

1 pound ground beef
1 teaspoon salt
⅛ teaspoon pepper
1 tablespoon finely chopped parsley
4 thinly sliced large onion rings
4 thin tomato slices
4 thin slices American cheese, cut 3 inches square

Mix the ground beef with the salt, pepper, and parsley. Shape mixture into 8 patties, 4 inches in diameter. On each of 4 patties arrange an onion ring, a tomato slice, and a slice of the cheese. Cover with the other 4 patties, and press edges together to seal. Broil on both sides for a total of about 20 minutes. Makes 4 servings.

## Ground Beef and Walnut Patties

Walnuts add flavor and crunchy texture to these ground beef patties.

1 pound ground beef
1 can (3 or 4 oz.) chopped mushrooms
½ cup chopped walnuts
¾ teaspoon salt
¼ teaspoon celery salt
¼ teaspoon pepper

Mix together the ground beef, mushrooms and liquid, chopped nuts, salt, celery salt, and pepper. Shape into 6 patties. Pan broil on an ungreased frying pan or griddle until brown and cooked to taste. Makes 6 servings.

## Hamburgers with Lemon Sauce

When you spoon the lemon-tomato sauce over these hamburgers, it sinks right in and flavors each patty.

1 onion, finely chopped
2 tablespoons butter or margarine
½ cup finely sliced celery
½ cup catsup
1 cup water
6 tablespoons lemon juice
3 tablespoons Worcestershire
2 tablespoons vinegar
2 tablespoons brown sugar
½ teaspoon salt
¼ teaspoon pepper
1½ teaspoons dry mustard
2 pounds ground beef

Sauté onion in butter until golden. Add the celery, catsup, water, lemon juice, Worcestershire, vinegar, brown sugar, salt, pepper, and mustard. Simmer for 15 minutes, or until the flavors are blended and celery is just tender. Shape ground beef into 8 patties, and broil or grill to desired doneness. Serve lemon sauce over patties. Makes 8 servings.

## Bacon-wrapped Blue Cheese Burgers

This juicy, cheese-flavored hamburger has a fat frankfurter shape—and you serve it accordingly, in a "hot dog" bun.

35 small blue-cheese-flavored crackers
   (about 1¼ cups)
½ cup milk
1 pound lean ground beef
1 small onion, minced
1 teaspoon salt
½ teaspoon monosodium glutamate
¼ teaspoon pepper
6 slices bacon
6 frankfurter buns

Soak crackers in milk until soft. Combine with beef, onion, salt, monosodium glutamate, and pepper. Divide meat mixture into 6 portions, and form each into a frankfurter shape. Spiral-wrap with bacon; secure with a toothpick. Broil until bacon is crisp and meat is as done as desired. Serve in warm buns. Makes 6 servings.

## Burgundy Burgers

Red wine and Roquefort cheese glorify these barbecued hamburgers.

¾ pound ground chuck
2 tablespoons chopped parsley
2 tablespoons minced green onion
¾ teaspoon salt
Freshly ground pepper to taste
⅓ cup Burgundy wine
Roquefort or blue cheese

Mix together ground chuck, parsley, green onion, salt, and pepper. Shape into 2 patties, making a depression in the center of each one. Place in a shallow pan, and pour wine over patties, pouring it into the depressions. Chill for 2 hours or longer. Broil over medium hot coals for 8 to 10 minutes for medium rare. Place a square of the cheese on each meat patty just before serving so it will melt slightly. Makes 2 servings.

## Hamburger and Eggplant Sandwich (see suggested menu below) *

1 medium-sized eggplant
Flour seasoned with salt and pepper
4 tablespoons bacon fat
¾ pound ground beef
1 small onion, minced
¼ cup fine dry bread crumbs
¼ cup water
2 tablespoons chopped parsley
½ teaspoon salt
¼ teaspoon pepper
⅛ teaspoon cinnamon
Butter
1 can (8 oz.) tomato sauce

Cut eggplant into 8 crosswise slices. Coat on both sides in seasoned flour. In a frying pan, quickly brown eggplant slices on both sides in bacon fat. Keep warm in oven.

Combine ground beef, onion, bread crumbs, water, parsley, salt, pepper, and cinnamon. Form mixture into 4 patties, each about the size of an eggplant slice. Fry patties in a small amount of butter until crisp and brown on both sides. To serve, place a meat patty between 2 eggplant slices. Pass heated tomato sauce. Makes 4 servings.

---

## * Hearty Supper for an Autumn Evening

Hamburger and Eggplant Sandwich (see recipe above)
Cracked Wheat Pilaff
Cucumbers in Sour Cream
Sugar-Crusted Broiled Fruits

For a hearty entrée for an evening meal, use sautéed eggplant slices to enclose a well-seasoned hamburger patty in a sandwich-like arrangement. The cucumber salad requires a few minutes of preparation ahead of time, but you can start the rest of the meal only 30 minutes before serving time.

### Cracked Wheat Pilaff
Cook according to directions on package of quick-cooking cracked wheat.

### Cucumbers in Sour Cream
¼ cup sour cream (or yogurt)
½ teaspoon garlic salt
½ teaspoon minced fresh mint, or ¼ teaspoon crushed dried mint
2 cucumbers, peeled and thinly sliced

Mix sour cream with garlic salt and mint. Mix gently but thoroughly with cucumber slices. Chill in refrigerator for 1 hour. Makes 4 servings.

### Sugar-Crusted Broiled Fruits
2 pears, peeled, quartered, and cut in thin slices lengthwise
1 cup fresh or canned pineapple chunks
2 tablespoons butter
⅓ cup brown sugar

Arrange pear slices in bottom of greased pie pan. Arrange pineapple chunks over pears. Dot with butter, and sprinkle with brown sugar. Slip under broiler until fruits are heated through and sugar bubbles. Makes 4 servings.

## Tarragon Beef Burgers

*(see suggested menu below)* ✳

1½ pounds lean ground beef
1½ teaspoons salt
¼ teaspoon pepper
3 tablespoons instant toasted onions
3 tablespoons tarragon vinegar
6 hamburger buns
6 cheese slices
Avocado slices

*Tarragon, toasted onions, sliced avocados, cheese make this a de luxe version of a family favorite.*

Mix together ground beef, salt, and pepper. Shape into 6 patties and place in a shallow pan. Sprinkle meat with onions and vinegar. Bake in a moderately hot oven (375°); allow 12 to 15 minutes for rare, 20 minutes for medium, and 25 minutes for well done. Split, butter, and toast buns. Melt cheese on one half of each bun; place a hamburger patty on the other half, and top with slices of avocado. Makes 6 servings.

---

## ✳Favorite Family Supper

Tarragon Beef Burgers (*see recipe above*)
Toasted Hamburger Buns with Cheese
Sliced Avocados
Buttered Corn on the Cob    Green Salad
Pear Bars

This should please children and adults alike: juicy beef patties, seasoned with tarragon and crunchy toasted onions, served on toasted buns, and teamed with corn on the cob and melted butter. Use your oven to brown the beef cakes and bake the dessert while you prepare the corn and salad. Fresh pears are the basis of the dessert.

**Pear Bars**

2 cups biscuit mix
⅔ cup milk
2 to 2½ cups thinly sliced pears (peeled and cored)
½ cup brown sugar, firmly packed
½ cup flour
1 package (3 oz.) cream cheese

Measure biscuit mix into a bowl. Add milk; stir until well mixed, and spread in a well-buttered 9-inch square pan. Arrange pear slices on top of dough. Mix together until crumbly the brown sugar, flour, and cream cheese. Strew crumbly mixture over pears. Bake in a moderately hot oven (375°) for 40 minutes. Cut into rectangles; serve warm or cold. Makes 6 to 8 servings.

## Meat Patties for the Freezer

It's a good idea to mix up some meat patties to keep on hand in the freezer. If you cook for two, you may want to make 3 packets of 2 patties each.

2 pounds lean ground beef
2 tablespoons water
2 teaspoons seasoned salt
½ teaspoon seasoned pepper

In a bowl, mix together well the beef, water, seasoned salt, and pepper. Divide into 6 parts, and shape each into a patty about 4 inches in diameter. Stack the patties, separating with a double thickness of waxed paper; wrap well in foil and freeze. Makes 6 servings.

To serve, remove from freezer and thaw for 30 to 45 minutes. Grill, broil, or fry, and serve in your favorite way.

## Cheeseburger Turnovers

Biscuits form the buns for these cheeseburger turnovers.

¾ pound ground beef
¼ teaspoon salt
Dash of pepper
1 package (8 oz.) refrigerator biscuits
2½ slices American cheese
3 tablespoons pickle relish
1 small onion, thinly sliced (optional)

Shape ground beef into 5 patties, each about 4 inches in diameter. Sauté over medium heat until browned on both sides and done to your liking. Season with salt and pepper. Remove from heat.

On a lightly floured board, roll each biscuit into a 5-inch round. Place each patty on a biscuit, and cover with ½ slice of cheese. Spread with pickle relish, and top with a few slices of onion, if you wish. Cover with one of the remaining biscuits; moisten edges with water and pinch to seal. Prick top of biscuits two or three times. Place on an ungreased baking sheet and bake in a moderately hot oven (375°) for 15 to 18 minutes, or until browned. Serve with mustard, if you wish. Makes 5 servings.

## Fruited Hamburgers with Wine Sauce

A tangy fruit and wine sauce dresses up these beef patties.

1 pound ground beef
1 teaspoon salt
¼ teaspoon pepper
½ teaspoon allspice
1 large green-tipped banana, sliced
2 slices bacon

*Wine sauce:*
1 teaspoon cornstarch
½ cup rosé wine
1 tablespoon lemon juice
2 teaspoons Worcestershire
½ teaspoon dry mustard
Salt and freshly ground pepper to taste
¼ cup orange marmalade

Mix meat with salt, pepper, and allspice. Shape into 4 patties. Broil until brown on one side, about 4 minutes; turn and cover each patty with a thin layer of sliced bananas and a half strip of bacon. Reduce oven temperature to 350° and continue to broil until bacon is crisp and bananas are soft, about 5 to 6 minutes longer. Meanwhile, in a small saucepan dissolve cornstarch in a small amount of wine. Combine with remaining wine, lemon juice, Worcestershire, mustard, salt and pepper to taste, and marmalade. Simmer uncovered until slightly thickened and clear, stirring frequently. Makes 4 servings.

## Soy-dipped Hamburgers  *(see suggested menu below)* ✳

½ cup soy sauce
½ cup water
1 clove garlic, crushed
2 teaspoons grated fresh ginger
2 tablespoons Worcestershire
6 tablespoons brown sugar
3 pounds lean ground beef
8 long French rolls
Thinly sliced tomatoes
Sliced green pepper

Combine soy sauce, water, garlic, ginger, Worcestershire, and brown sugar. Shape ground beef into 8 log-shaped meat patties (to fit the long French rolls). Pour marinade over the meat and marinate for 1 to 1½ hours. Cook meat over hot coals, or broil, until done to your liking. Split rolls and toast them on the grill or in the broiler. Fill with the meat patties, thinly sliced tomatoes, and sliced green pepper. Makes 8 servings.

## ✳ Family Picnic Barbecue

Soy-dipped Hamburgers *(see recipe above)*
Sour French Rolls
Sliced Green Peppers      Sliced Tomatoes
Marinated Bean Salad
Peach Pie
Favorite Beverages

Everything on this menu travels easily and is especially suitable for carrying and serving from plastic containers. Make the salad the day before so it has time to marinate. Buy or make the peach pie. Slice the peppers and tomatoes. Shape the hamburgers and place in a container with lid, make the marinade and pour over just before leaving home. At the picnic, grill the meat over charcoal until done to your liking. Take along your favorite beverages, iced tea or coffee, soft drinks, or lemonade.

### Marinated Bean Salad

1 can (1 lb.) red kidney beans, drained
1 can (8 oz.) cut green beans, drained
1 can (1 lb.) garbanzo beans, drained
1 can (1 lb.) black-eyed beans, drained
2½ cups chopped celery
1 cup finely minced parsley
1 bunch green onions, chopped
1 small jar (3 oz.) stuffed green olives, halved
1 can (3 oz.) chopped black olives

½ cup salad oil or olive oil
½ cup red wine vinegar
1 teaspoon salt
⅛ teaspoon pepper
2 tablespoons brown sugar
1 clove garlic, mashed
Romaine

Combine kidney beans, green beans, garbanzo beans, and black-eyed beans. Rinse beans with water. Drain and mix in a bowl with celery, parsley, green onions, green olives, and black olives. Combine salad oil, vinegar, salt, pepper, brown sugar, and garlic. Pour over bean mixture. Mix lightly, cover, and refrigerate overnight. Toss mixture well and arrange in bowl lined with crisp romaine. Makes about 8 servings.

## Opera Sandwich

*Ooperavoileipä*, or Opera Sandwich, is a Finnish version of the hamburger. It's a slice of French bread toasted in butter, topped with a grilled patty of very lean ground beef, which in turn is topped with a fried egg.

2 pounds very lean ground beef
½ cup finely chopped onion
1½ teaspoons salt
¼ teaspoon pepper
2 tablespoons butter
6 thick slices French bread, buttered on both sides
6 eggs

In a bowl, combine ground beef with onion, salt, and pepper; mix until ingredients are thoroughly blended. Divide mixture into 6 portions, shape each into an oval patty. Melt butter in a heavy frying pan, add meat patties, and grill on both sides until done to your liking. Preferably, the center should still be pink.

In another frying pan or griddle, toast French bread slices over medium heat until golden on both sides; remove from pan and keep hot. Use the same pan to fry the eggs until whites are congealed but yolks are still soft. Place a cooked meat patty on each slice of hot bread, and top each with a fried egg. Serve immediately. Makes 6 servings.

## Liverburgers

Lemon juice adds a subtle seasoning to this mixture of meats. One trick: Liver is easier to grind while it is still frozen.

1 pound frozen liver
1 pound ground beef
2 teaspoons salt
¼ teaspoon pepper
1 tablespoon lemon juice

Force frozen liver through a food grinder and combine with ground beef, salt, pepper, and lemon juice. Form into 8 thick patties and brown slowly on both sides on a lightly greased griddle or in a heavy frying pan. Makes 8 servings.

*You top toasted French bread with a patty of lean ground beef and a fried egg to make an Opera Sandwich.*

## Barbecued Cheeseburgers

Barbecue these ground beef and cheese stacks to serve alone or to fit between split toasted buns for a husky sandwich.

2 pounds lean ground beef
2 tablespoons minced dried onions
2 teaspoons Worcestershire
2 teaspoons prepared mustard
1 teaspoon salt
½ teaspoon pepper
1½ cups shredded sharp Cheddar cheese

Thoroughly mix together the ground beef, onions, Worcestershire, mustard, salt, and pepper. Shape into 12 thin patties. Put ¼ cup of the shredded cheese in a mound on top of each of 6 of the patties; top each with another meat patty and press edges together to seal. Grill over hot coals to your liking (about 5 minutes each side for medium). Baste with melted butter; turn only once. Makes 6 servings.

## Watercress Beef Patties Oriental Sauce

These unusual beef patties are light in texture, with spicy watercress adding its flavor in a subtle but definite manner. They are served with a sesame-soy sauce that is rich and exotic. If you wish, garnish the beef patties with sprigs of watercress when you serve them.

1 pound ground beef
½ teaspoon salt
⅛ teaspoon pepper
½ teaspoon allspice
½ cup fine dry bread crumbs
¾ cup finely chopped watercress leaves
¼ cup water
3 tablespoons butter or margarine
2 tablespoons toasted sesame seed
2 tablespoons sherry
1 tablespoon soy sauce
2 teaspoons Worcestershire

Combine the ground beef with the salt, pepper, allspice, bread crumbs, watercress, and water. Form into six patties. Brown slowly on both sides in 1 tablespoon of the butter to the doneness you prefer. Remove meat to a serving plate and keep warm. Lightly brown the remaining 2 tablespoons butter in the pan in which the meat was cooked. Add the sesame seed, sherry, soy sauce, and Worcestershire. Bring to a boil and pour sizzling hot over the meat on the serving plate. Makes 3 servings.

## Coffee-glazed Hamburger Patties

Coffee gives a flavor surprise to these hamburgers.

1 pound ground beef
1 egg
½ cup rolled oats
1 medium-sized onion, finely chopped
1 can (8 oz.) tomato sauce
1 teaspoon salt
¼ teaspoon pepper
⅛ teaspoon garlic salt
½ cup catsup
½ cup cold coffee

Mix together thoroughly the ground beef, egg, rolled oats, onion, tomato sauce, salt, pepper, and garlic salt. Shape into 8 patties. Brown meat quickly on both sides in a hot, ungreased frying pan; pour off pan drippings. Stir the catsup into the coffee, then pour over browned cakes. Simmer gently for 20 minutes, or until meat is cooked and sauce has thickened. Turn patties occasionally so they will be glazed on both sides. Makes 4 servings.

## Sweet and Sour Hamburgers

This ground beef dish is tasty and attractive, and the simplicity of the recipe is an added reason for serving it often.

1 pound ground beef
½ pound bulk pork sausage
1 teaspoon salt
⅛ teaspoon pepper
1 large onion, sliced
2 tablespoons soy sauce
½ cup water
¼ cup vinegar
½ cup brown sugar

Mix the ground beef, sausage, salt, and pepper together and form into 6 large patties. Brown on both sides in an ungreased frying pan. Add the sliced onion. Mix together the soy sauce, water, vinegar, and brown sugar and pour over. Cover and simmer until hamburgers and onions are done, about 15 minutes. Makes 6 servings.

## Broiled Beef Steaks with Onion Gravy *(see suggested menu below)* ✳

1½ pounds lean ground beef
1 tablespoon lemon juice
1½ teaspoons salt
½ teaspoon pepper
1 package (1 oz.) onion gravy mix, or 1 package brown gravy mix and 2 teaspoons instant minced onion
¼ cup red wine

Combine the beef with lemon juice, salt, and pepper; mix well. Shape into 6 oblong steaks about ¾ inch thick. Broil 4 to 5 minutes per side about 6 inches from broiler (cook longer if you prefer them well done). Prepare onion or brown gravy mix as directed on the package, substituting wine for ¼ cup of the water. Serve the beef patties topped with onion gravy. Makes 6 servings.

---

## ✳ Low-Calorie Dinner for Six

Broiled Beef Steaks with Onion Gravy *(see recipe above)*
Cucumber Salad
Broiled Tomatoes Parmesan
Sesame Seed Crackers
Pineapple with Honey Sauce

An eye-appealing and satisfying meal need not be overladen with calories, as this dinner menu illustrates. It is complete from appetizer to dessert but still below a calorie count of 600 per person. It can be prepared in a short time since the recipes are simple.

### Cucumber Salad

3 medium-sized cucumbers
½ teaspoon salt
1½ cups low-fat cottage cheese
3 tablespoons vinegar
1 tablespoon minced parsley
1 tablespoon minced green onion top
⅛ teaspoon pepper
Lettuce
Parsley

Peel, halve lengthwise, and slice cucumbers. Place in a bowl and sprinkle with salt; set aside. In the container of an electric blender (or in the small bowl of an electric mixer), combine the cottage cheese, vinegar, parsley, green onion, and pepper. Whirl (or mix) until well blended. Mix with cucumbers; chill. Serve on lettuce leaves and garnish with parsley. Makes 6 servings.

### Broiled Tomatoes Parmesan

6 medium-sized tomatoes
Salt and pepper
2 tablespoons grated Parmesan cheese
1½ teaspoons butter

Halve tomatoes crosswise; sprinkle with salt and pepper. Then sprinkle about ¼ teaspoon Parmesan over each tomato half; dot each with ¼ teaspoon butter. Broil for 4 to 5 minutes about 6 inches from broiler. Makes 6 servings of 2 halves each.

### Pineapple with Honey Sauce

1 medium-sized fresh pineapple
2 teaspoons honey
1 cup yogurt
Mint leaves for garnish

Peel pineapple and cut into bite-size chunks; refrigerate in a covered bowl. Stir honey into yogurt; chill. When ready to serve, arrange chunks in six sherbet dishes, top with the sauce, and garnish each serving with a mint leaf. Makes 6 servings.

# Triple-seasoned Hamburger  (see suggested menu below) *

1 round loaf French bread
Butter
2 pounds ground beef
1 tablespoon chili sauce
1 teaspoon salt
1 teaspoon prepared mustard
Pepper
Blue cheese
Paprika
Lemon juice

Slice French bread loaf in half crosswise, making top and bottom slices. Butter the cut surfaces and heat. Combine ground beef, chili sauce, salt, and mustard. Form into a large patty. Pan-broil on one side; turn. As second side browns, season top side with a layer of pepper, then a layer of blue cheese crumbles, then a sprinkling of paprika. Drizzle with lemon juice. When done, place between French bread slices. Cut in wedges to serve. Makes 6 servings.

# * Teen-agers' Party

Triple-seasoned Hamburger (see recipe above)
Assorted Pickles and Relishes
Patio Salad
Baked Beans        Potato Chips
Panocha-Pecan Cake Fingers

A teen-ager often decides to entertain on short notice. Here's a menu that can be prepared quickly—and it's easy on the cook, too. We suggest you feature a favorite—hamburger—but try the novel seasoning teen-agers recommend: Sprinkle it with pepper till it's black, blue cheese crumbles till it's white, paprika till it's red, then squeeze on plenty of lemon juice.

## Patio Salad

4 carrots, shredded
1 cup pitted dates, cut into pieces
1 can (1 lb., 9 oz.) pineapple chunks, drained
1 cup sliced celery
½ cup sour cream
Lettuce

Mix together carrots, dates, pineapple chunks, and celery. Chill. At serving time, toss with sour cream. Serve from lettuce-lined bowl. Makes 6 to 8 servings.

## Panocha-Pecan Cake Fingers

1 package yellow cake mix
½ cup brown sugar, firmly packed
¼ cup butter
¼ cup heavy cream
1 cup chopped pecans

Make yellow loaf cake (about 9 by 12 inches) from packaged mix, according to package directions. Cool slightly. Boil together to soft ball stage (238° on candy thermometer) the brown sugar, butter, and cream. Pour over top of cake. Sprinkle with chopped pecans. Cut cake into squares. Makes 12 servings.

## Mexican Meat Patties

Here Mexican flavors add interest to grilled hamburger patties. Canned tamales, green chili sauce, and frozen tortillas make this dish a quick one.

1 small can (about 7 oz.) beef tamale
1 pound ground beef
2 tablespoons milk
1 teaspoon chili powder
½ teaspoon salt
¼ teaspoon garlic salt
6 large corn tortillas, fresh or frozen and defrosted
2 tablespoons butter
1 can (7 oz.) green chili sauce (salsa)

Turn the tamale into a bowl and mash well with a fork. Add beef, milk, chili powder, salt, and garlic salt. Shape into 4 large patties and broil until done to your liking. Meanwhile cut the tortillas into strips ¼ inch wide. Melt butter in a large heavy frying pan; add tortilla strips and cook quickly, stirring with a fork, until they are soft and lightly browned, 3 to 4 minutes. Turn out on a warm serving dish; top with the broiled patties. Heat chili sauce to serve on meat and tortillas. Makes 4 servings.

## Smoky Ground Beef Cakes

Liquid smoke and bacon give an "outdoor taste" to broiled ground beef patties.

1½ pounds ground beef
1 egg
½ cup finely chopped onion
1 teaspoon salt
½ teaspoon pepper
1 teaspoon sage
1½ teaspoons liquid smoke
6 slices bacon

Combine the ground beef with the egg, onion, salt, pepper, sage, and liquid smoke; then shape into 6 thick cakes. Wrap one slice of bacon around the outside of each cake, and secure with toothpick; chill. Broil slowly until brown on both sides. Makes 6 servings.

## Meat Patty Skillet

Brown sugar and vinegar give a mild sweet-sour flavor to these ground meat patties and sautéed onion slices.

1 pound ground beef
2 cups soft bread crumbs
¼ cup chopped onion
½ cup water
1 teaspoon salt
⅛ teaspoon nutmeg
⅛ teaspoon powdered thyme
4 large onions, cut in thick slices
2 tablespoons butter or margarine
¼ cup brown sugar, firmly packed
2 tablespoons water
½ teaspoon dry mustard
¼ cup vinegar

Combine meat, bread crumbs, chopped onion, the ½ cup water, salt, nutmeg, and thyme. Shape into 8 patties. Sauté sliced onions in melted butter or margarine until tender and lightly browned. Remove from saucepan. In the same pan, brown patties on both sides. Return onions to pan. Combine brown sugar with the 2 tablespoons water, mustard, and vinegar, and mix thoroughly. Pour over meat and onions. Cover and simmer slowly for 35 minutes. Makes 8 servings.

*Delicately flavored Meat Balls in Tomato Sauce (page 24) are delicious over hot spaghetti. Breadsticks, a green salad, and Cherry Crunch dessert complete the meal.*

# MEAT BALLS

## *these are different*

---

### Spanish Meat Balls with Cracked Wheat

These meat balls simmer in a peppery tomato sauce. They are particularly good over steamed cracked wheat.

½ cup dried mushrooms
1 cup warm water
1 large onion, chopped
1½ cloves garlic, minced or mashed
¼ cup olive oil or salad oil
2 cans (1 lb., 13 oz. each) tomatoes
¾ teaspoon salt
6 small dried hot chili peppers
2 pounds ground beef (or a mixture of ground beef, veal, and pork)
½ cup fine dry bread crumbs
1 medium-sized onion, finely chopped
1½ teaspoons chopped parsley
¾ teaspoon salt
¼ teaspoon white pepper
2 eggs
5 to 6 cups hot steamed cracked wheat

Soak mushrooms in the 1 cup water. Sauté the chopped large onion and garlic in oil until transparent. Add the tomatoes, the soaked dried mushrooms (cut in pieces), the mushroom liquid, ¾ teaspoon salt, and chili peppers (thread chili peppers on a string so they can easily be removed). Simmer for 1 hour.

Mix together thoroughly the ground meat, bread crumbs, the chopped medium onion, parsley, salt, and pepper. Beat eggs slightly and mix in. Shape into balls about the size of a walnut. Add to the sauce and simmer slowly for 1 hour longer. Remove the string of chili peppers before serving. To serve, spoon meat balls and sauce over cracked wheat. Makes 8 to 10 servings (about 40 meat balls).

### Almond Meat Balls

Almonds, cheese, and mustard seed go into these meat balls.

1½ pounds ground beef
½ pound ground pork
2 eggs
½ cup milk
1 tablespoon mustard seed
2 teaspoons salt
½ teaspoon pepper
1 small clove garlic, minced or mashed
½ cup chopped almonds
12 salted soda crackers
¼ pound processed Cheddar cheese
2 cans (1 lb. each) tomatoes
2 cans (8 oz. each) Spanish-style tomato sauce
2 small onions, sliced
½ teaspoon salt
½ teaspoon pepper
Hot cooked egg noodles

Mix together the ground meats, eggs, milk, mustard seed, 2 teaspoons salt, ½ teaspoon pepper, and garlic. Put almonds, crackers, and cheese through the fine blade of the food chopper; mix thoroughly with the meat mixture. Roll into balls about the size of a walnut, and place in a 3-quart casserole. Combine tomatoes, tomato sauce, onion, ½ teaspoon salt, and ½ teaspoon pepper; pour over meat balls. Cover and bake in a moderate oven (350°) for 1 hour. Serve over hot cooked noodles. Makes 6 servings.

## Meat Balls with Rice and Celery

Asparagus soup lends color and a surprising curry-like flavor to this full-meal dish. The celery retains its crispness.

1 pound ground beef
½ cup rolled oats
½ teaspoon salt
½ teaspoon pepper
½ teaspoon celery salt
1 teaspoon dried parsley
3 tablespoons butter or margarine
1 cup uncooked rice
1½ cups sliced celery
1 large onion, chopped
1 can (6 or 8 oz.) mushroom stems and pieces
1 teaspoon salt
2 cans (10½ oz. each) cream of asparagus soup
2 cups water

Mix together the ground beef, rolled oats, ½ teaspoon salt, pepper, celery salt, and parsley. Roll meat into balls the size of a medium-sized walnut; brown on all sides in butter or margarine. Arrange half the browned meat balls in the bottom of a greased 3-quart casserole. Cover with a layer of rice, celery, and onion, and add the remaining meat balls. Spoon mushrooms and juice on top. Sprinkle with the 1 teaspoon salt. Pour asparagus soup and water over all. Cover and bake in a moderate oven (350°) for 1 hour, or until liquid is absorbed and rice is tender. Makes 6 servings.

## Meat Balls and Beans

These juicy meat balls cook with Mexican beans for an excellent transfer of flavors.

2 cups pink (Mexican) dried beans
Water
1 tablespoon salt
1 pound ground beef
½ pound ground pork
¾ cup rolled oats or fine dry bread crumbs
1 teaspoon salt
Pepper to taste
½ cup evaporated milk
1 medium-sized green pepper, chopped
1 medium-sized onion, sliced

Wash beans; cover with water and simmer for 2½ hours, or until tender. Just before beans are tender, add the 1 tablespoon salt. Mix together thoroughly the ground meats, rolled oats or crumbs, the 1 teaspoon salt, pepper, and evaporated milk; form into balls about 1½ inches in diameter. Drop meat balls into the beans; add the green pepper and sliced onion. Cover and simmer for 45 minutes. Mash 1 cup of the beans and return to pan to thicken the broth. Makes 8 servings.

## Meat Balls with Capers

Just two tablespoons of capers contribute the distinctive flavor of these meat balls.

2 pounds ground chuck
1 small onion, finely chopped
2 tablespoons capers, drained and chopped
1 tablespoon minced parsley
1 egg, slightly beaten
½ teaspoon pepper
½ teaspoon ground ginger
2 teaspoons salt
2 tablespoons salad oil or shortening
¼ cup flour
1 tablespoon brown bottled gravy sauce
1 cup water
Hot cooked rice or noodles

Combine the ground chuck with the onion, capers, parsley, egg, pepper, ginger, and 1 teaspoon of the salt. Form lightly into small balls. Heat the salad oil in a large frying pan and brown the meat balls, rolling from side to side until evenly browned; remove meat balls. Stir into the fat in the pan the flour mixed with the remaining 1 teaspoon of salt. Gradually stir in the gravy sauce and water, stirring until gravy is thickened. Return meat balls to gravy and simmer for about 10 minutes. Serve over hot cooked rice or noodles. Makes 6 servings.

# German Meat Balls

These fluffy meat balls absorb some of the cream gravy as they bake.

1½ pounds ground beef
½ pound ground pork
¼ cup finely chopped onion
1 egg
½ cup fine dry bread crumbs
2 cups light cream
1 teaspoon salt
¼ teaspoon pepper
1½ teaspoons brown sugar
½ teaspoon allspice
¼ teaspoon nutmeg
¼ cup flour (more if needed)
¼ cup (4 tablespoons) butter or margarine
Paprika

Combine ground beef, ground pork, and onion. Beat egg lightly and mix into the meat mixture with bread crumbs, 1 cup of the cream, salt, pepper, brown sugar, allspice, and nutmeg. Shape into small balls 1¼ inches in diameter, and roll in flour. Brown on all sides in melted butter in a moderately hot frying pan—about 10 minutes total time. Pour remaining 1 cup of cream over meat balls; cover, and simmer slowly for 10 to 15 minutes. Makes 6 to 8 servings.

# Indian Meat Balls

Here's a recipe for tiny meat balls made in an electric frying pan. While the meat balls simmer in their rich gravy, you can assemble the rest of your menu.

1½ pounds ground chuck
¼ cup finely chopped onion
½ cup chopped celery
¾ cup crushed bran flakes
2 tablespoons butter or margarine
1 large onion, chopped
¾ teaspoon sugar
⅛ teaspoon pepper
¾ cup water
3 tablespoons soy sauce

Mix together the meat, ¼ cup onion, celery, and bran flakes. Form into about 18 balls. With your electric frying pan set at medium heat (340°), melt butter and brown meat balls on all sides. Combine large onion, sugar, pepper, water, and soy sauce. Pour over meat, cover, and cook over low heat (225°) for 45 minutes. Makes 4 to 6 servings.

# Parsley Meat Balls

You can shape this parsley and onion-seasoned meat in small balls for hors d'oeuvres, or in larger balls for an entrée.

¾ cup fine dry bread crumbs
½ cup milk
2 onions, chopped
½ cup water
2 pounds ground chuck
¾ cup finely chopped parsley
3 mint leaves, chopped
2 egg yolks
3 small cloves garlic, minced or mashed
1½ teaspoons salt
¼ teaspoon pepper
1½ tablespoons olive oil
1½ tablespoons butter
¼ cup red wine vinegar or lemon juice
½ teaspoon crumbled dried oregano

Soak bread crumbs in milk; then beat until mushy. Cook onions, covered, in the water until water has boiled away. Mix together thoroughly the meat, soaked bread crumbs, onions, parsley, mint, egg yolks, garlic, salt, and pepper. Form into walnut-sized balls. Heat oil and butter, and brown meat balls on all sides, slowly and well. Transfer meat balls to a serving dish. Pour wine vinegar into the pan, heat, and scrape up drippings; pour over meat balls. Sprinkle with oregano. Makes 3 dozen small meat balls.

# Frikadeller (Danish Meat Balls)

This is a good recipe to cook for a crowd; the meat balls can be made the previous night and reheated.

1⅔ pounds lean ground beef
⅓ pound ground pork
1 small onion
2 or 3 eggs
4½ tablespoons flour
1½ teaspoons salt
¼ teaspoon pepper
2½ to 3 cups milk
Hot shortening or bacon drippings

Ask your meat man to grind the meat twice, fine grind. At home, grind the meat and onion together in a meat grinder 2 times. Mix in eggs, flour, salt, and pepper. Add milk, a little at a time, until mixture is of the right consistency to shape with a spoon into soft balls the size of a small egg. Scoop up meat balls one by one with a tablespoon dipped in the hot shortening, and drop into hot shortening to brown (dip the spoon in the shortening again before picking up each meat ball). Fry meat balls until done and well browned. Set aside and prepare sauce.

*Sauce:*
1 large jar (10 oz.) large Spanish-style green olives
2 cups water
1 cup dry sherry
1 tablespoon grated onion
3 bouillon cubes
6 tablespoons butter
6 tablespoons flour

Drain liquid from olives and save to use in sauce. Slice green olives into slivers and set aside. Combine olive liquid, water, sherry, grated onion, and bouillon cubes in a saucepan. (The amount of sherry can be varied to suit your preference. If you like a darker gravy, color with gravy concentrate.) Boil until bouillon cubes are dissolved. Melt butter in pan; blend in flour. Slowly add hot liquid mixture, stirring continually. When this is thick and of gravy consistency, stir in previously sliced olives. Add salt and pepper to taste, if desired (remember that green olives are salty). This should make about 3 cups of gravy. Place meat balls in gravy, and reheat slowly. Makes about 12 servings (60 meat balls).

# Greek Meat Balls

These are outstanding. If you plan to serve them with spaghetti, double the sauce recipe.

4 slices French bread
1 cup water
2 pounds ground beef
1 small onion, grated or finely chopped
¼ cup cracker meal
1 cup finely chopped parsley
1 tablespoon salt
¼ teaspoon celery seed
½ teaspoon pepper
½ teaspoon monosodium glutamate
¼ cup grated Parmesan cheese
3 eggs
Flour (approximately 2 cups)
Olive oil or salad oil
½ bottle of catsup
2 cups water

Remove crusts from French bread; pour the 1 cup water over bread and let stand until bread absorbs moisture. Combine bread, ground beef, chopped onion, cracker meal, parsley, salt, celery seed, pepper, monosodium glutamate, cheese, and eggs. Work ingredients with your hands until soft and well blended. Drop meat mixture, a tablespoon at a time, into flour; roll each ball in flour until all the moist spots disappear. Into a heavy frying pan, pour olive oil to a depth of ½ inch; heat oil until you can brown a bread cube in 1 minute. Brown meat balls, a few at a time, turning only once. Remove and keep warm until all meat balls are browned.

Pour off half of the olive oil left in the frying pan. To the remainder add the catsup and the 2 cups of water, and bring to a boil; add meat balls. Cover, and simmer gently for 30 minutes, turning meat balls only once. Makes 10 servings.

## Meat Balls with Buttermilk Sauce *(see suggested menu below)* ✱

1½ pounds ground beef
1 small onion, finely chopped
3 tablespoons chopped green pepper
⅓ cup sliced celery
1 cup cooked rice
1 teaspoon salt
½ teaspoon pepper
1 egg
1 can (10½ oz.) mushroom soup
1 soup can of buttermilk
1 can (2 oz.) mushroom stems and pieces

Place in a large bowl the ground beef, onion, green pepper, celery, rice, salt, pepper, and egg; work together with your hands until well mixed. Divide meat into 12 portions and roll each into a ball. Place in a greased 2-quart casserole. Place the mushroom soup, buttermilk, and liquid from mushrooms in a bowl; beat until smooth. Pour over meat balls, along with mushrooms. Bake in a moderate oven (350°) for 1 hour. Makes 6 servings.

---

## ✱ *Scandinavian Supper*

Wilted Lettuce and Tomatoes
Meat Balls with Buttermilk Sauce *(see recipe above)*
Mashed Potatoes
Fresh Peas with Dill Butter Sauce
Chilled Olallieberry Soup      Sweet Cream

The flavor touches in this supper menu are typically Scandinavian.

### *Wilted Lettuce and Tomatoes*

4 cups lettuce leaves, broken into pieces
3 tomatoes, peeled (not chilled) and cut into thin wedges
Salt and freshly ground pepper to taste
½ cup (¼ pound) butter
3 tablespoons sesame seed

Place lettuce leaves in salad bowl. Add tomato wedges. Sprinkle with salt and pepper. Slowly heat butter with sesame seed until butter is lightly browned. Pour hot butter over lettuce and tomatoes and quickly cover. After 2 minutes, remove cover, toss, and serve. Makes 4 to 6 servings.

### *Fresh Peas with Dill Butter Sauce*

4½ pounds fresh peas, shelled
Boiling salted water
4 tablespoons finely chopped dill pickle
⅓ cup melted butter
Salt and pepper

Cook peas in boiling salted water for 8 minutes or just until tender; drain. Heat chopped dill pickle in melted butter. Season with salt and pepper, and pour over the cooked peas. Toss lightly and serve immediately. Makes 4 to 6 servings.

### *Olallieberry Soup*

1 cup water
Sugar to taste (about ⅔ cup)
4 cups fresh olallieberries (or any tart berry such as boysenberry, raspberry, or loganberry)
1½ tablespoons cornstarch
2 tablespoons water
Sweet cream

Combine the 1 cup water and the sugar in a saucepan; bring to a boil. Add berries; bring to a boil again. Cook for 1 or 2 minutes, taking care that berries do not overcook and fall apart. Blend cornstarch with the 2 tablespoons water. Stir into berry mixture. Stirring gently, bring to a boil again. Allow to cool; chill. Serve in sherbet glasses. Pass sweet cream. Makes 4 to 6 servings.

## Lemon Meat Balls

Lemon juice, stuffed green olives, a band of crisp bacon on the outside, and a filling of cheese inside make these meat balls distinctive. The ease in preparation makes them an excellent party dish.

¼ pound sharp Cheddar cheese
½ green pepper
12 pimiento-stuffed green olives
1 pound ground beef
1 cup fine dry bread crumbs
1 egg
½ cup milk
3 tablespoons lemon juice
1 teaspoon salt
6 slices bacon

Grind cheese, green pepper, and olives together in food chopper. Combine with ground beef, and add bread crumbs, egg, milk, lemon juice, and salt. Mix thoroughly. Roll ingredients into 12 balls, wrapping each ball with ½ slice of bacon. Secure tightly with toothpicks. Arrange on a shallow baking pan, and bake in a hot oven (400°) for 30 minutes. Makes 6 servings.

## Beef-Wheat Balls

Freshly ground wheat accentuates the meat flavor of these herb-seasoned meat balls. Serve them over hot buttered noodles or rice.

1 pound ground beef
¾ cup cracked wheat
½ cup finely chopped onion
1 teaspoon salt
2 tablespoons minced parsley
¼ teaspoon mixed herbs (thyme, marjoram, and basil)
2 tablespoons chopped walnuts
2 cans (10½ oz. each) beef bouillon
2 soup cans water
1½ cups sour cream
Hot buttered noodles or rice

Mix together thoroughly the ground meat, cracked wheat, onion, salt, parsley, herbs, and nuts. Roll into balls about the size of small walnuts. In a large kettle, bring to a boil the beef bouillon and water; drop in meat balls, cover, and simmer just until the balls rise to the top (about 15 minutes). Remove meat balls from broth and mix with sour cream. Serve over hot buttered noodles or rice. Makes 8 to 10 servings (about 40 meat balls).

## Norwegian Meat Balls

Tender meat balls, chilled overnight in a wine sauce, are superb party fare.

1 pound each lean sirloin and lean pork, ground with a small piece of suet
3 thin slices day-old bread, crumbled
1 small onion, chopped
2 eggs, beaten
1 teaspoon salt
1 teaspoon cornstarch
¼ teaspoon allspice
Black pepper
¼ cup evaporated milk
¼ cup salad oil
3 tablespoons flour
1 can (10½ oz.) beef bouillon
1 cup water
1 cup Burgundy
Hot cooked noodles

With a very, very light hand, using a fork so you don't crush the meat, mix meats, bread, onion, eggs, salt, cornstarch, allspice, pepper, and milk. Scoop up meat mixture with a round-bowled spoon; drop into oil heated in frying pan; turn to brown all sides. Remove meat balls to platter, and make sauce in same pan.

Stir flour into oil remaining in the frying pan and stir until it begins to brown. Add liquids slowly, stirring sauce until smooth and thickened. Place meat balls in sauce, cover, and simmer for 30 minutes. Chill in refrigerator overnight to set the flavors. Heat meat balls and serve on noodles. Makes 6 to 8 servings.

# Mexican Meat Balls

This meat ball dish is spicy hot; reduce the chili powder by a teaspoonful if you prefer it less so. Because you don't have to brown the meat balls before adding them to the sauce, this is an easy recipe to cook for a crowd.

1 pound ground beef
½ cup fine dry bread crumbs
1 medium-sized onion, finely chopped
2 cloves garlic, minced or mashed
1 teaspoon ground coriander seed
1½ teaspoons salt
½ teaspoon pepper
2 eggs, slightly beaten
1 can (1 lb.) tomatoes
1 can (8 oz.) tomato sauce
1 medium-sized onion, chopped
1 clove garlic, minced or mashed
1 tablespoon chili powder
Hot buttered noodles, rice, cracked wheat,
  or polenta

Mix together thoroughly the ground beef, bread crumbs, 1 onion, 2 garlic cloves, coriander, salt, pepper, and eggs. Shape into balls about 1¼ inches in diameter. Into a large kettle with a tight-fitting cover, put the tomatoes, tomato sauce, 1 onion, 1 garlic clove, and chili powder; cover and simmer for 5 minutes. Drop meat balls into the hot tomato sauce, cover, and simmer for 45 minutes. Serve over hot buttered noodles, rice, cracked wheat, or polenta. Makes 6 servings.

# Yummy Balls

These are adaptable. If anyone is late to dinner, it doesn't matter a bit, and if any meat balls are left over (which is doubtful), they are almost better warmed over than when first made.

1 pound ground beef
½ pound ground lean pork
1 small onion, minced
½ cup uncooked rice
½ cup cracker crumbs
1 egg
½ teaspoon salt
Pepper to taste
1 can (10½ oz.) tomato soup
1 soup can water

Mix ground meats, onion, rice, cracker crumbs, egg, and seasonings. Shape into balls about the size of golf balls, and place in a greased casserole. Pour over tomato soup diluted with water. Bake in a moderately hot oven (375°) for 1 hour. Makes 6 servings.

# Spinach Meat Balls

Their moist, light texture makes these well-seasoned meat balls distinctive.

1 package (10 oz.) frozen chopped spinach
1 pound ground beef
1 medium-sized onion, grated
1 egg
¾ teaspoon salt
⅛ teaspoon pepper
¾ cup flour
2 tablespoons salad oil, butter, or margarine
1 can (10½ oz.) cream of mushroom soup
⅓ cup sherry or consommé

Cook spinach as directed on the package; drain well. Mix together spinach, meat, onion, egg, salt, and pepper; roll into small balls. Roll in flour until thoroughly coated. Heat oil in frying pan, and brown meat balls on all sides. Add mushroom soup and sherry. Cover and simmer for 1 hour. Makes 4 to 6 servings.

## Meat Balls in Tomato Sauce *(see suggested menu below)* *

1 pound lean ground beef
¼ pound ground veal
¼ pound ground pork
1 clove garlic, minced or mashed
½ cup fresh bread crumbs
¼ cup milk
1 egg, slightly beaten
2 teaspoons salt
½ teaspoon pepper
Flour
4 tablespoons olive oil or salad oil
1 large onion, chopped
2 cans (1 lb. each) tomatoes, chopped
1 tablespoon chopped parsley
½ teaspoon oregano
½ teaspoon sugar
3 tablespoons tomato paste
Cooked spaghetti

Mix together until lightly blended the ground beef, veal, pork, garlic, bread crumbs, milk, egg, 1½ teaspoons of the salt, and ¼ teaspoon of the pepper. Shape into 2-inch meat balls. Dredge in flour; brown on all sides in the olive oil. Remove from pan and set aside.

In the same pan, brown the onion, stir in tomatoes, parsley, oregano, and sugar. Add tomato paste, remaining ½ teaspoon salt, and ¼ teaspoon pepper. Simmer, stirring occasionally, for 15 minutes. Stir in the browned meat balls and simmer, stirring occasionally, for 15 minutes longer. Place some of the hot cooked spaghetti on each plate and pour some of the meat balls and sauce over each serving. Makes enough meat and sauce for 4 to 6 servings.

---

## * Spaghetti and Meat Ball Dinner

Meat Balls in Tomato Sauce (*see recipe above*)
Hot Spaghetti        Breadsticks
Mixed Green Salad
Cherry Crunch

The delicately flavored meat balls in this menu combine veal, pork, and beef. For a hearty family meal, serve them in a rich tomato sauce over hot cooked spaghetti, accompanied by bread sticks and your favorite green salad. You can bake the dessert ahead of time. Serve it warm, either plain or with cream or ice cream.

### Cherry Crunch

1 cup quick-cooking rolled oats
½ cup flour
1 cup sugar
½ cup butter or margarine
1 can (about 1 lb.) cherry pie filling
Cream or ice cream (optional)

Combine oats, flour, and sugar; cut in butter until mixture is crumbly. Place half of the mixture in the bottom of a buttered 8-inch square baking pan; spoon in pie filling, then spread remaining crumb mixture over the top. Bake in a moderate oven (350°) for 45 minutes, or until lightly browned. Serve warm. Spoon into sauce dishes and top with cream or ice cream, if you wish. Makes 6 servings.

## Swedish Meat Balls

These may be served from a chafing dish or electric skillet.

1 cup soft bread crumbs, firmly packed
1 cup milk
1 pound each thrice-ground pork and beef
3 eggs
½ cup finely grated onion
2 teaspoons salt
Pepper and allspice to taste
1 cup milk
Flour
2 tablespoons salad oil or shortening
2 cans (10½ oz. each) consommé

Soak bread crumbs in 1 cup milk. Mix together thoroughly, using an electric mixer or rotary beater, the ground pork and beef, eggs, soaked bread crumbs, grated onion, salt, pepper, and allspice. Beat at slow speed, and gradually add the other 1 cup milk; continue beating until very smooth; chill thoroughly. Drop meat mixture by spoonfuls onto floured waxed paper, roll into balls with floured hands, brown a few at a time in shortening or oil. Pour in consommé, cover, and simmer for 20 minutes. Makes 12 to 14 servings.

## Cabbage Leaf Meat Balls in Foil

Both cabbage leaves and foil seal the juiciness into this steaming, savory meat mixture.

¾ pound lean ground beef
⅓ cup soft bread crumbs
¾ teaspoon salt
Dash of pepper
¼ cup chopped canned tomatoes
1 small onion, finely chopped
½ cup cooked rice
8 large cabbage leaves
Salt
Boiling water

Mix together ground beef, crumbs, salt, pepper, tomatoes, onion, and rice. Form into 16 small balls. Wash cabbage leaves thoroughly; trim off thick part of each. Sprinkle with salt; pour boiling water over the leaves to wilt. Allow to drain well. Then wrap 2 meat balls in each of the leaves, folding in from four sides, envelope fashion. Place each bundle in center of a 12-inch square of foil. Bring foil corners together; twist slightly. Bake on a baking sheet in a moderately slow oven (325°) for 45 minutes. Makes 4 servings.

## Baked Kotleti

Austrians have a special way of preparing meat balls. Their trick of folding stiffly beaten egg whites into the meat mixture results in a pleasingly light and tender meat ball. Pass a bowl of sour cream when you serve this savory meat dish.

3 pounds ground chuck
6 tablespoons butter or margarine
2 teaspoons salt
½ teaspoon freshly ground pepper
2 tablespoons minced parsley
6 slices stale bread
4 eggs, separated
4 tablespoons flour
2 cups canned consommé
6 tablespoons sour cream

Add to the ground meat 2 tablespoons softened butter, salt, pepper, and parsley. Soak bread in water, squeeze nearly dry, and tear up finely; add to the meat mixture, along with egg yolks; mix thoroughly. Whip egg whites until stiff, but not dry, and fold in, stirring with a fork. Form meat mixture into 2 dozen oval-shaped patties. Sauté in the remaining butter until browned on each side. Transfer to a casserole.

Stir flour into the drippings and brown slightly, then stir in consommé; bring to a boil. Stir in sour cream, blending until smooth, and pour over the meat balls. Bake in a moderate oven (350°) for 25 minutes. Makes 10 servings.

## Meat Balls in Sweet and Sour Sauce

These meat balls simmer in a tangy sweet and sour sauce.

2 pounds lean ground beef
1 cup fresh bread crumbs
¼ cup milk
1 egg, slightly beaten
1 medium-sized onion, chopped
1 green pepper
1 clove garlic, minced or mashed
1 teaspoon salt
¼ teaspoon pepper
1½ teaspoons soy sauce
2 tablespoons salad oil
2 tablespoons cornstarch
¼ cup cider vinegar
½ teaspoon ground ginger
½ cup soy sauce
½ cup water
¼ cup brown sugar, firmly packed
1 can (13½ oz.) pineapple tidbits
1 cup sliced celery
Hot cooked rice

Mix together until lightly blended the ground beef, bread crumbs, milk, egg, onion, ½ of the green pepper (finely chopped), garlic, salt, pepper, and 1½ teaspoons soy sauce. Shape into balls about 1 inch in diameter. Brown in oil on all sides. In a large pan blend cornstarch with vinegar until smooth. Add ginger, the ½ cup soy sauce, water, and brown sugar. Cook, stirring occasionally, until thickened. Stir in pineapple (including syrup), celery, and remaining ½ green pepper (sliced). Add meat balls; simmer, stirring occasionally, for 20 minutes. Serve with hot cooked rice. Makes 6 to 8 servings.

## Meat Balls Romashko with Black Sauce

These unusual meat balls, wrapped in spinach leaves, are moist, savory, and well seasoned. The sauce is spicy and slightly sweet.

6 medium-sized fresh mushrooms, chopped
1 medium-sized onion, chopped
1 green pepper, chopped
2 tablespoons butter
1½ pounds ground chuck
1 linguisa (Portuguese sausage; about 4 oz.),
    skinned and chopped
2 slices white bread, without crusts,
    soaked in water
1 teaspoon monosodium glutamate
2 eggs
¼ teaspoon *fines herbes*
1 can (1 lb.) tomatoes, with liquid
    drained off and reserved
1 bunch fresh spinach (with large leaves)
Shortening

Sauté mushrooms, onion, and pepper in butter until onion is transparent. Mix with all remaining ingredients except spinach and shortening. Form into golf-ball-sized balls and brown quickly in hot shortening. Cool. Wrap each ball in a spinach leaf (stem removed) that has been wilted in hot water. Set carefully in a 2-quart casserole.

*Sauce:*
10 large dried prunes, seeded and chopped
2 teaspoons chopped fresh ginger root, or
    1 teaspoon powdered ginger
1 tablespoon Worcestershire
1 can (8 oz.) tomato sauce
1 tablespoon salt
½ teaspoon pepper, or to taste
1 teaspoon chicken stock concentrate or
    beef stock concentrate
6 medium-sized fresh mushrooms, sliced
Reserved liquid (about 1 cup) from can of tomatoes
1 cup dry red wine
1 cup water

Combine all ingredients except wine and water, and simmer for 10 to 15 minutes. Pour over meat balls and add wine and water to cover. Bake in a moderately hot oven (375°) for 30 to 45 minutes. Makes 6 to 8 servings (about 24 meat balls).

## Meat Balls in Bean Sauce

A rich, black bean sauce surrounds these spiced meat balls.

1 pound ground chuck (preferably put through grinder twice)
1 cup fine dry bread crumbs
1 teaspoon salt
¼ teaspoon pepper
Dash of allspice
Dash of nutmeg
1 egg, beaten
1 cup milk
1 small onion, finely minced
3 tablespoons olive oil or salad oil
1 can (10½ oz.) black bean soup
1 cup milk
Hot steamed rice
Finely chopped parsley

Mix together thoroughly the ground meat, bread crumbs, salt, pepper, allspice, nutmeg, egg, 1 cup milk, and onion. Shape into small balls about the size of a walnut. Heat oil and brown meat balls on all sides. Pour in the black bean soup mixed with 1 cup milk. Cover and simmer for 1 hour. Serve over hot steamed rice. Sprinkle with parsley. Makes 4 to 6 servings.

## Caraway Meat Balls Supreme

Caraway is definitely, and purposely, dominant in these tender meat balls.

1 tablespoon caraway seed
1 tablespoon instant minced onion
3 tablespoons red wine vinegar
1 pound ground beef
½ pound bulk pork sausage
1½ cups soft bread crumbs
¾ cup milk
1 egg
1½ teaspoons salt
¼ teaspoon coarse-ground pepper
Flour
2 tablespoons salad oil
1 cup hot water

In a large bowl, soak caraway seed and onion in wine vinegar for 10 minutes. Add beef, sausage,

bread crumbs, milk, egg, salt, and pepper; mix thoroughly. Shape into balls the size of large walnuts, roll in flour, and brown in hot oil. Lower heat and simmer for 10 minutes. Add hot water. Cover; simmer for 30 minutes. Makes 8 servings (about 32 balls).

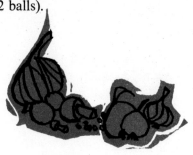

## Meat Balls in Sour Cream Gravy

Dill and ripe olives flavor these meat balls. Sour cream goes in the sauce to make a rich, creamy gravy.

2 cups cornflakes
1 pound ground beef
½ cup milk or beef stock
1 teaspoon salt
⅛ teaspoon pepper
2 tablespoons finely chopped onion
10 pitted ripe olives
1½ tablespoons shortening or salad oil
1½ tablespoons flour
¼ cup water
½ teaspoon dill seed
1 cup (½ pint) sour cream
Hot buttered noodles

Crush cornflakes into fine crumbs. Combine with ground beef, milk or beef stock, salt, pepper, and onion. Mix lightly until blended. Shape each meat ball around an olive. In a frying pan, heat shortening or salad oil. Put in meat balls; cook, turning to brown on all sides. When browned, remove meat balls from pan. Pour off all but 2 tablespoons of the drippings. Blend in flour until smooth.

Gradually stir in water; cook, stirring constantly, until thickened and smooth. Add dill seed. Add the meat balls. Reduce heat; cover and simmer for 15 minutes. Stir in sour cream; heat just to the boiling point. Serve over hot buttered noodles. Makes about 3 servings.

## Meat Balls in Tangy Sauce

The unusual thing about these meat balls is the distinctive beer flavor of the sauce.

3 slices dry bread
¾ cup warm water
2 pounds ground chuck
1 egg
2 cloves garlic, finely chopped
1 medium-sized onion, finely chopped
2 tablespoons Worcestershire
1 teaspoon salt
½ teaspoon pepper
¼ cup olive oil or salad oil
1 package dry onion soup mix (amount for
   3 or 4 servings)
1 can (12 oz.) beer
1 cup (½ pint) sour cream
Hot cooked rice

Soak dry bread in water. In a bowl combine the meat, egg, garlic, onion, Worcestershire, salt, pepper, and soaked bread. Blend well and form into about 30 balls. In a frying pan, heat the oil. Add meat balls and cook over medium heat until well browned on all sides. Sprinkle onion soup mix over meat balls. Add beer; cover and simmer for 10 minutes. Add sour cream; mix and heat just until well blended and heated through. Serve with hot cooked rice. Makes 6 to 8 servings.

## Miniature Meat Balls

A subtle blending of ingredients and long, slow cooking combine to give these meat balls their outstanding flavor.

2 pounds lean ground beef
1 pound bulk pork sausage
1 cup fine dry bread crumbs
2 tablespoons grated or chopped onion
1 teaspoon salt
¼ teaspoon pepper
2 eggs
½ cup dry red wine
Flour
2 tablespoons bacon drippings
1 can (6 or 8 oz.) mushroom stems and pieces
   or whole mushrooms

In a large bowl, mix together meat, bread crumbs, onion, salt, pepper, eggs, and about half of the wine. Form mixture into small balls about the size of a medium-sized walnut. Roll in flour and brown in the bacon drippings in a heavy frying pan. Remove, place in a roasting pan or casserole with a tight-fitting cover. Pour fat from frying pan over the meat balls and add the remaining wine and the liquid from the mushrooms. Cover tightly and cook in a moderate oven (350°) for 2 hours.

One hour before serving, add the mushrooms. Just before serving, remove meat balls and thicken gravy with flour, adding water as necessary to make enough gravy to go around. Makes 6 to 8 generous servings.

## Twice-cooked Hamburger Balls

This recipe turns out meat balls with a very fine texture and a crisp crust.

1 pound ground beef
1 clove garlic, minced
1 small onion, chopped
1 bouillon cube
½ cup hot water
1 teaspoon salt
¼ teaspoon pepper
1 tablespoon soy sauce
1 teaspoon Worcestershire
¼ teaspoon dried thyme
3 eggs
¾ cup fine dry bread crumbs
1 can (10½ oz.) cream of mushroom soup
½ cup water

Crumble beef into heavy frying pan and sauté lightly to bring out the fat, but do not brown. Add garlic and onion and sauté until tender. Drain off excess fat. Dissolve bouillon cube in water and add with seasonings; cool to lukewarm. Add 2 of the eggs and the bread crumbs. Chill until firm. Form into balls about the size of a walnut. Beat the other egg, roll balls in egg and then in bread crumbs. Fry in deep fat (390°) until browned. Heat mushroom soup and water together. Pour over meat balls just before serving. Makes 6 servings.

## Curry Meat Balls  (see suggested menu below) *

3 pounds ground beef
1½ teaspoons salt
½ teaspoon pepper
1 tablespoon salad oil
2 medium-sized onions, chopped
1 cup sliced celery
¼ cup (4 tablespoons) butter or margarine
2 to 3 teaspoons curry powder
4 tablespoons dry sherry
2 teaspoons sugar
2 tablespoons minced parsley
2 beef bouillon cubes dissolved in 2 cups hot water
3 tablespoons cornstarch
¼ cup water
Cooked rice

Season ground beef with salt and pepper; shape meat into walnut-sized balls. Brown in oil in a large frying pan; cover and turn heat to low and cook for about 15 minutes, turning with a fork occasionally to prevent burning. Remove from pan, and set aside.

In the same pan, sauté onion and celery in butter until limp. Stir in curry, sherry, sugar, parsley, and bouillon; simmer for about 7 minutes, stirring occasionally. Dissolve cornstarch in ¼ cup cold water to make a paste. Bring sauce mixture to a gentle boil; add cornstarch paste; stir contantly until the mixture is thickened. Spoon meat balls into the sauce, cool to room temperature, then cover and refrigerate for 3 to 5 hours. Reheat over medium heat, stirring, until heated through (about 5 minutes). Serve with rice. Makes 6 to 8 servings.

---

## * A Simple Dinner for Guests

Curry Meat Balls (see recipe above)
Rice      Buttered Limas
Tropical Cabbage Salad
Walnut Torte

Meat balls in a curry sauce are the basis for this dinner. You make them ahead and reheat them just before serving. The walnut dessert can also be made early in the day. Make the salad and cook the limas just before serving.

### Tropical Cabbage Salad

1 medium-sized head cabbage
1 cup flaked coconut
¾ cup sour cream
2½ tablespoons vinegar
¾ teaspoon salt
¼ teaspoon pepper
1 tablespoon sugar
Toasted coconut
Paprika

Finely shred cabbage. Add flaked coconut. Blend together sour cream, vinegar, salt, pepper, and sugar. Toss lightly with cabbage and coconut. Sprinkle with toasted coconut and paprika. (To toast coconut, spread a thin layer on a baking sheet and toast in a 350° oven for 3 or 4 minutes until lightly browned, watching carefully and stirring when necessary.) Makes 6 to 8 servings.

### Walnut Torte

3 eggs
1 cup sugar
1 cup crushed graham cracker crumbs
½ cup chopped walnuts
Currant jelly
Whipped cream

Beat eggs until thick and lemon colored. Add sugar, crumbs, and nuts; mix well. Pour batter into a greased and floured 9-inch cake pan. Bake in a moderate oven (350°) for 25 minutes, or until torte tests done when you insert a cake tester. Cool in pan. Turn onto serving dish and spread top with a layer of jelly; top with whipped cream. Cut in wedges. Makes 6 to 8 servings.

# MEAT LOAVES

## *make them plain or make them fancy*

---

## *Meat Loaf with Cranberry Wine Sauce*

The scarlet-colored fruit and wine sauce gives this meat loaf a refreshing tang.

1½ pounds ground beef
1 can (12 oz.) pork luncheon meat, ground
2½ cups soft bread crumbs, well packed
2 tablespoons minced onion
Salt and pepper to taste
¾ cup milk
2 eggs, slightly beaten
½ cup dry red table wine
½ cup brown sugar, firmly packed
1 can (1 lb.) whole cranberry sauce
¼ teaspoon ground cloves
1 tablespoon cornstarch

Mix together thoroughly the ground beef and ground luncheon meat, bread crumbs, onion, salt and pepper to taste, milk, and eggs. Shape into a 9 by 4-inch loaf and place in a greased baking pan.

Mix together the wine and brown sugar; mix in cranberry sauce and cloves. Spread ¾ of the cranberry mixture over the top of the meat loaf, and set aside the remaining cranberry mixture.

Bake in a moderate oven (350°) for 1 hour, basting several times with the sauce. Remove meat loaf to a hot platter. Blend together the cornstarch and the reserved cranberry mixture. Stir into the drippings left in the pan, and cook until the sauce is thick. Slice meat loaf and serve with the sauce. Makes 6 to 8 servings.

## *Beef and Pork Loaf*

For a substantial sandwich meal, serve thick slices of this meat loaf on thin slices of French bread, drizzled with the tart-sweet tomato glaze.

1 cup cracker crumbs
1 medium-sized onion, finely chopped
1½ pounds lean ground beef
½ pound ground pork
2 teaspoons salt
2 teaspoons Worcestershire
⅛ teaspoon pepper
⅛ teaspoon sage
¼ teaspoon poultry or sausage seasoning
2 eggs, slightly beaten
1 can (8 oz.) Spanish-style tomato sauce

*Tomato glaze:*
1 teaspoon prepared mustard
3 tablespoons brown sugar
¼ teaspoon nutmeg
¼ cup catsup

Mix together the cracker crumbs, onion, beef, pork, salt, Worcestershire, pepper, sage, poultry seasoning, egg, and tomato sauce. Pat mixture into a shallow baking pan (about 5 by 13 by 3 inches). Combine ingredients for tomato glaze, and pour one-third of the glaze evenly over the loaf. Bake in a moderate oven (350°) for 1 hour. Serve hot or cold, sliced, with the remaining tomato glaze served separately to spoon over individual portions. Makes 8 servings.

---

*For a patio meal, try moist, well-seasoned meat loaf baked inside a crunchy loaf of French bread and served with a spicy tomato sauce to spoon over each serving (page 35). Bread case keeps meat hot for some time.*

## Stuffed Meat Loaf

The bread stuffing in the center of this rolled loaf absorbs flavor from the cooking meat.

1½ pounds lean ground beef
¾ pound ground pork
1½ teaspoons salt
¼ teaspoon pepper
1 egg

*Stuffing:*
½ cup seedless raisins
4 cups toasted bread cubes
⅓ cup minced onion
2 tablespoons minced parsley
¼ teaspoon sage
¼ teaspoon pepper
¾ teaspoon salt
⅔ cup hot meat broth or water

Mix together the beef, pork, salt, pepper, and egg. On a sheet of waxed paper, pat meat mixture evenly to form a square about ½ inch thick. Toss together until well mixed, the raisins, bread, onion, parsley, sage, pepper, salt, and broth. Pat in an even layer over the meat. Roll as for a jelly roll and place in a baking pan seam side down. Bake in a moderate oven (350°) for 1½ hours. Serve sliced, hot or cold. Makes 8 servings.

## Vegetable Meat Loaf

This moist meat loaf with crisp bits of carrot, celery, and green onion is good served either hot or cold.

1½ cups cubed French bread or rye bread
1 cup milk
2½ pounds ground chuck
2½ teaspoons salt
¼ teaspoon pepper
1 cup chopped green onion,
   including some of the tops
½ cup grated raw carrot
⅓ cup chopped celery
2 hard-cooked eggs, finely diced
1 tablespoon freshly grated or prepared horseradish
⅛ teaspoon salt
½ cup heavy cream, whipped

In a bowl combine the bread cubes with milk; let stand for about 1 hour, or until the bread is very soft. Add the meat, the 2½ teaspoons salt, pepper, green onion, carrot, celery, and hard-cooked eggs. Mix lightly until well blended. Turn into a loaf pan (about 9 by 5 by 3 inches) or shape into a loaf on a shallow baking pan. Do not pack the meat mixture. Bake in a moderate oven (350°) for 1 hour. Serve with horseradish cream sauce made by blending together the horseradish, the ⅛ teaspoon salt, and the cream. (Or serve with prepared horseradish, if you prefer.) Makes 6 to 8 servings.

## Cottage Cheese Meat Loaf

Because you bake this light-textured meat loaf in a shallow pan instead of a loaf pan, the baking time is cut to 30 minutes.

1 pound ground beef
1 cup (½ pint) cottage cheese
1 egg
½ cup quick-cooking rolled oats
¼ cup catsup
1 tablespoon prepared mustard
2 tablespoons chopped onion
1 teaspoon salt
⅛ teaspoon pepper
⅓ cup grated Parmesan cheese

Combine the ground beef with the cottage cheese, egg, rolled oats, catsup, prepared mustard, onion, salt, and pepper. Mix the ingredients lightly until well blended. Press the mixture loosely into a shallow baking pan (about 8 inches square). Bake in a moderate oven (350°) for 20 minutes. Remove from oven and sprinkle the Parmesan cheese evenly over the top. Return to the oven and continue to bake for 10 minutes longer. Let stand for about 5 minutes before cutting in squares to serve. Makes 6 servings.

## Ground Beef Roast

The zip in this baked beef dish comes from the sliced lemon, green pepper, and onion arranged over the top.

1½ pounds ground beef
4 slices bread
½ cup milk
½ cup chopped parsley
1 tablespoon melted butter or margarine
1 egg, beaten
1 teaspoon salt
Pepper to taste
2 teaspoons soy sauce
½ teaspoon monosodium glutamate
½ lemon, sliced very thin
1 green pepper, sliced crosswise
1 large onion, sliced thin and broken into rings
¾ cup catsup
¼ cup water
1 tablespoon butter

Combine meat with bread that has been soaked in the milk. Mix in parsley, butter, egg, salt, pepper, soy sauce, and monosodium glutamate. Pat meat into a cake about 1 inch thick, in a greased 10-inch round baking dish. Cover the top evenly with the lemon slices, green pepper, and onion. Mix catsup with water, pour over onion rings, and dot with butter. Bake in a hot oven (450°) for 30 minutes. Makes 6 servings.

## Barbecued Beef Loaf

Here's an exceptionally good way to barbecue ground beef. The meat remains moist and stays together surprisingly well, and it's easy to check the degree of doneness by making a small knife cut in the center of the loaf.

1 pound ground round or ground sirloin
1 egg
1 clove garlic, pressed
2 pieces bacon
½ cup soy sauce

Mix beef with egg and garlic. Mold into a loaf 2 inches thick, 6 inches long, and 3 inches wide. Wrap bacon around loaf near ends; tie string loosely over each piece. Pour soy sauce over loaf;

*Sliced lemon, green pepper, and onion rings give a zesty topping to Ground Beef Roast (recipe at left).*

let stand for about 10 minutes. Turn loaf in soy; let stand for another 10 minutes. Cook over a medium fire for 25 minutes (for medium rare), or slightly longer until meat is done to your liking. Makes 2 to 4 servings.

## Beef and Spinach Loaf

Horseradish is particularly good with this meat and vegetable loaf.

1 pound ground beef
2 packages (10 oz. each) frozen chopped spinach, cooked and well drained
1 medium-sized onion, grated or very finely chopped
1 cup cooked rice
2 teaspoons salt
¼ teaspoon pepper
2 eggs, slightly beaten
3 slices bacon
Prepared horseradish

Mix together ground beef, spinach, onion, rice, salt, pepper, and eggs. Pack into a greased 9 by 5-inch loaf pan. Arrange bacon over the top. Bake in a moderate oven (350°) for 1 hour, or until firm. Serve with horseradish. Makes 6 to 8 servings.

## Frosted Meat Loaf with Raisin Sauce (see suggested menu below) *

1½ pounds ground beef
½ cup shredded carrot
¼ cup finely chopped parsley
1 cup fine dry bread crumbs
1 cup tomato juice
1 egg, slightly beaten
1 teaspoon salt
½ teaspoon pepper
2 teaspoons sugar
2 teaspoons Worcestershire
2 slices bacon

*Sweet potato frosting:*
3 cups hot mashed sweet potatoes
1 egg
⅓ cup milk
½ teaspoon salt
1 tablespoon brown sugar
½ teaspoon cinnamon

*Raisin sauce:*
⅓ cup each finely chopped onion, finely chopped
    green pepper, and finely chopped celery
1 clove garlic, minced or mashed
3 tablespoons butter or margarine
½ cup seedless raisins
⅓ cup catsup (the kind with
    additional chili seasoning)

1 teaspoon cornstarch
1 cup water
1 tablespoon lemon juice
2 tablespoons sugar
¼ teaspoon liquid hot-pepper seasoning
1 teaspoon prepared mustard
½ teaspoon salt
Dash of pepper

Mix together the ground beef, carrot, parsley, bread crumbs, tomato juice, egg, and seasonings. Pat into a buttered 9 by 5-inch loaf pan; top with bacon slices. Bake in a moderately hot oven (375°) for 1 hour. Drain off any fat; turn meat loaf onto a heatproof platter or board, and frost with a mixture of the mashed sweet potatoes, egg, milk, salt, brown sugar, and cinnamon. Place in a very hot oven (500°) for 20 minutes or until lightly browned.

Make raisin sauce: Simmer onion, green pepper, celery, and garlic in butter for 5 minutes. Stir in raisins, catsup, cornstarch which has been blended with the water, lemon juice, sugar, liquid hot-pepper seasoning, mustard, salt, and pepper. Cook slowly for 20 minutes. (Sauce can be reheated.)

Serve meat loaf, sliced, with raisin sauce. Makes 6 generous servings.

---

## * Family Dinner or Simple Buffet for Guests

Frosted Meat Loaf with Raisin Sauce (*see recipe above*)
Cabbage and Peas Casserole
Rolls      Butter
Hot Chocolate Sundae

You can easily adapt this family dinner to a buffet style meal when you entertain. It features meat loaf frosted with mashed sweet potatoes and served with a raisin sauce. The vegetable casserole can be made early in the day and cooked or reheated just before serving. For dessert, top scoops of chocolate or coffee ice cream with warmed chocolate sauce.

### Cabbage and Peas

8 cups shredded cabbage (about 1 medium-sized
    head)
3 quarts boiling salted water
½ cup fresh or frozen peas
¾ cup light cream

Cook cabbage in boiling salted water for about 10 minutes or until tender; drain. Mix cooked cabbage with peas and cream in a 2-quart casserole. Cover and bake in a moderately hot oven (375°) for 8 to 10 minutes. Makes 6 to 8 servings.

## Meat Loaf with Prunes

This meat loaf has a center layer of prunes, and a spicy sauce, prepared separately, to spoon hot over each serving.

1 medium-sized onion, finely chopped
2 tablespoons butter or margarine
1½ pounds lean ground beef
1 large can (4½ oz.) deviled ham
2 eggs
½ cup soft bread crumbs
½ cup milk
1 teaspoon sugar
1 teaspoon salt
¼ teaspoon pepper
2 tablespoons chopped parsley
1 cup cooked, pitted prunes
3 slices bacon

*Spiced sauce:*
1 cup liquid from cooked prunes (or prune juice)
Grated peel from 1 lemon or orange
1½ tablespoons lemon juice
1½ tablespoons tarragon vinegar
½ cup brown sugar, firmly packed
1 tablespoon prepared mustard
1 teaspoon cinnamon
¼ teaspoon allspice
¼ teaspoon cloves
2 tablespoons melted butter or margarine
2 tablespoons flour

Cook onion in butter until soft. Mix thoroughly with beef, deviled ham, eggs, bread crumbs, milk, sugar, salt, pepper, parsley. Pat half of the mixture into a loaf pan (about 5 by 9 inches); arrange a layer of prunes; cover with remaining meat, patting firmly in place; top with bacon. Bake in a moderate oven (350°) for 1 hour.

For the sauce, combine prune liquid, lemon peel, lemon juice, vinegar, brown sugar, mustard, cinnamon, allspice, and cloves. Bring to a boil and simmer for 10 minutes. Blend melted butter with flour, blend with some of the hot sauce, then combine with sauce in pan and cook, stirring, until thickened. Serve meat loaf hot or cold, sliced, with hot spiced sauce over each portion. Makes 8 servings.

## Meat Loaf in a Loaf

Moist, well-seasoned meat loaf is baked inside a crunchy loaf of French bread. After the loaf bakes, the crust is crisp but not difficult to cut or eat. The bread case also keeps the meat hot for some time, which makes this a good dish for outdoor meals.

1 round loaf French bread
1 tall can evaporated milk
1 small onion, minced
1 small green pepper, seeded and chopped
1 pound ground beef
1 egg, slightly beaten
1¼ teaspoons salt
½ teaspoon pepper
½ teaspoon monosodium glutamate
Hot spicy tomato sauce (optional)

Cut a thin slice from the top of the French bread. Scoop out the inside of the loaf. Measure out 2 cups of the bread crumbs and soak in the evaporated milk for 10 minutes. Add the onion, green pepper, ground beef, egg, salt, pepper, and monosodium glutamate. Work with your hands until thoroughly mixed. Fill bread case with the meat mixture; put the top slice back in place. Place on a lightly greased pan and bake in a moderate oven (350°) for 1 hour and 15 minutes. Serve hot, with or without tomato sauce, or cold. Makes 6 to 8 servings.

## Mushroom-stuffed Meat Loaf

The meat loaf encases a savory mushroom and onion stuffing for this good looking, yet inexpensive, company entrée.

½ pound medium-sized mushrooms, sliced
1 large onion, chopped
½ cup finely sliced celery
2 tablespoons butter or margarine
¾ cup tomato juice
1 cup soft bread crumbs
1½ teaspoons salt
⅛ teaspoon pepper
2 pounds ground chuck
2 eggs

Sauté mushrooms, onion, and celery in butter until vegetables are limp. Add ½ cup of the tomato juice, and simmer for 10 minutes. Mix in bread crumbs, ½ teaspoon of the salt, and pepper. Mix ground meat with remaining 1 teaspoon salt, remaining ¼ cup tomato juice, and eggs. Shape meat mixture into a loaf in a greased baking dish; scoop out center, fill with mushroom mixture, and pat remaining meat mixture over mushroom stuffing, enclosing it completely with the ground meat. Bake in a hot oven (450°) for 20 minutes; reduce temperature to moderate (350°), and bake for 30 minutes longer. Makes 8 servings.

## Danish Cheese Meat Loaf

The caraway and cumin in Danish kuminost cheese are subtle in this mildly flavored meat loaf. Chili sauce gives the loaf a pinkish color and a slight sweetness; it tastes something like a ham loaf.

1½ pounds ground beef
1 cup fine dry bread crumbs
2 eggs, beaten
½ cup milk
1 cup chili sauce
½ cup (2 oz.) shredded Danish kuminost cheese
    with caraway and cumin seeds
½ teaspoon salt
¼ teaspoon freshly ground pepper

Mix together thoroughly the ground meat, bread crumbs, eggs, milk, chili sauce, grated cheese,

*When you slice what appears to be ordinary fare, a savory mushroom stuffing will delight your guests.*

salt, and pepper. Turn into a greased 5 by 9-inch loaf pan. Bake in a moderate oven (350°) for 50 minutes, or until nicely browned. Makes 8 servings.

## Ham-Beef Loaf

Here is a moist and fluffy meat loaf with a mild smoked ham flavor.

½ pound ham
1 small onion
1 pound ground beef
½ cup quick-cooking rolled oats
1 small can (2 oz.) mushroom stems
    and pieces, drained
½ can (4½ oz.) chopped ripe olives
1 egg, slightly beaten
1 small can (⅔ cup) evaporated milk
½ cup warm water

Grind ham and onion together in food chopper or blender. Add ground beef, rolled oats, mushrooms, olives, egg, and milk; mix thoroughly. Form into a loaf in baking pan, and pour over the warm water. Bake in a moderately slow oven (325°) for 1 hour and 15 minutes, basting occasionally with liquid in pan. Allow to cool for about 15 minutes before slicing. Makes 6 servings.

# Chili Meat Loaf *(see suggested menu below)* ✳

1½ pounds ground beef
¾ cup cooked rice
¼ cup fine dry bread crumbs
1 egg, slightly beaten
½ cup milk
1 medium-sized onion, minced
½ cup sliced stuffed green olives
2 tablespoons raisins
1 tablespoon chili powder
½ teaspoon ground cumin seed
Salt and pepper to taste
1 green pepper, cut into thin rings
2 slices bacon, cut into 1-inch lengths
¾ cup catsup (the kind with
   additional chili seasoning)

Combine ground beef, rice, bread crumbs, egg, and milk. Mix thoroughly with onion, olives, raisins, chili powder, cumin seed, salt, and pepper. Lightly pat into a well-greased loaf pan (9 by 5 inches). Arrange green pepper rings and bacon slices over the top. Bake in a moderately hot oven (375°) for 45 minutes. Pour catsup over loaf, return to oven, and bake for 20 minutes more, until bubbly. Allow to stand for 10 minutes. Lift out onto a platter to slice and serve. Serve any juices and catsup remaining in the baking pan as a sauce. Makes 6 servings.

---

# ✳ Chili Meat Loaf Dinner

Fresh Vegetable Relish Tray
Chili Meat Loaf *(see recipe above)*
Fresh Green Beans with Buttered Green Onions
Hot Cornbread          Whipped Honey Butter
Raisin Nut Squares
Vanilla Ice Cream

Almost everyone likes a good meat loaf, and this dinner features an exceptional one, highly seasoned and almost like chili con carne in meat loaf form.

### Fresh Green Beans with Buttered Green Onions

1½ pounds fresh green beans
Boiling salted water
2 tablespoons finely minced green onions
¼ cup melted butter
Salt and pepper

Cook beans in boiling, salted water just until tender, about 20 minutes. Drain; turn into serving dish. Very slightly sauté green onions in the melted butter; pour over beans. Add salt and pepper to taste. Makes 6 servings.

### Raisin Nut Squares

1 egg
1 cup brown sugar, firmly packed
⅓ cup unsifted flour
¼ teaspoon salt
½ cup raisins
⅔ cup coarsely chopped walnuts

In the small bowl of your electric mixer, beat together the egg and brown sugar until light and fluffy. Add flour and salt, mixing until well combined. Stir in raisins and walnuts and turn into a buttered, 8 by 10-inch pan. Bake in a moderately hot oven (375°) for 15 to 20 minutes. Cool and cut into 6 servings. Serve with a topping of vanilla ice cream.

## Family Meat Loaf

*(see suggested menu opposite)* ✱

1½ pounds ground chuck
⅔ cup quick-cooking rolled oats
   or 1 cup fine dry bread crumbs
1 cup milk
1 teaspoon salt
⅛ teaspoon pepper
¼ teaspoon poultry seasoning
2 eggs
1 teaspoon Worcestershire
1 small onion, finely chopped

*Meat loaf glaze:*
¼ cup catsup
1½ to 2 tablespoons brown sugar
1 teaspoon prepared mustard
¼ teaspoon nutmeg (or less)

In a large mixing bowl, combine the ground chuck, rolled oats or crumbs, milk, salt, pepper, poultry seasoning, eggs, Worcestershire, and chopped onion. Put in a loaf pan (4½ by 8½ inches). Set aside while you prepare the glaze.

In a measuring cup, combine the catsup, brown sugar, mustard, and nutmeg. Spread over the meat loaf. Bake in a moderate oven (350°) for about 1 hour and 15 minutes. Makes 6 to 8 servings.

## Swedish Hamburger

Shape seasoned ground beef like a giant hamburger and bake at high heat to desired degree of doneness to make a refreshing version of meat loaf.

1½ pounds lean ground beef
1 egg
1 small onion, chopped
¼ cup chopped parsley
1 teaspoon salt
¼ teaspoon pepper

Mix together ground beef, egg, onion, parsley, salt, and pepper. Shape into a thick round cake like a large meat patty. Place in a small frying pan or shallow casserole (one just large enough to hold patty). Bake in a moderately hot oven (375°). Allow about 25 minutes for rare, 35 minutes for medium, and 45 minutes for well done. Cut in wedges to serve. Makes 4 to 6 servings.

*Toasted sesame seed is sprinkled over baked carrots that accompany this meat loaf (menu on opposite page).*

## Zucchini Meat Loaf

Zucchini and tomato both provide moisture in this well-seasoned meat loaf.

2 small zucchini
2 medium-sized onions
1 tablespoon salad oil
2 medium-sized tomatoes, peeled and chopped
¼ cup milk
1 slice day-old bread, torn into small pieces
1 egg
1 teaspoon Worcestershire
1 small clove garlic, mashed or minced
1 teaspoon salt
½ teaspoon pepper
1 pound ground beef
¼ pound ground pork

Run the unpeeled zucchini and onions through the food chopper; sauté in salad oil for 1 minute. Add tomatoes, and simmer until zucchini and onions are tender; cool. Heat milk to lukewarm, pour over bread, and let stand for 5 minutes. Beat egg, then stir into milk mixture with Worcestershire, garlic, salt, pepper, and vegetables. Combine with meat mixture and blend together thoroughly. Pack into a greased 9 by 5-inch loaf pan; let stand for at least 1 hour before baking so flavors blend. Bake in a moderately slow oven (325°) for 1½ hours. Let stand for 10 minutes before slicing. Makes 8 servings.

# * Meat Loaf Supper for the Family

Family Meat Loaf (*see recipe opposite*)
Baked Potatoes with Chive Topping
Sesame Carrots
Peach and Cottage Cheese Salad
Fresh Orange Sundae

In this menu, meat loaf, potatoes, and vegetables bake together while you assemble the simple salad. First ready the carrots for baking as directed below and set them aside. Start baking the potatoes while you mix the meat loaf, then put the loaf and the carrots in the oven with the potatoes. Prepare individual peach and cottage cheese salads. Make the sundaes just before you serve them.

## Baked Potatoes with Chive Topping

Scrub and grease 6 potatoes and place in a hot oven (400°); after 15 minutes reduce heat to 350° and continue to bake for about 1 hour and 15 minutes. Slit open the top of each potato and dress each with about 3 tablespoons commercial chive-flavored sour cream or potato topping. Makes 6 servings.

## Sesame Carrots

8 medium-sized carrots
Butter
2 tablespoons sesame seed
¼ teaspoon salt
Dash of pepper

Wash and peel carrots, and halve them lengthwise. Arrange carrots in a shallow casserole, dot with butter, and cover. Bake in a moderate oven (350°) for about 1 hour and 15 minutes, or until tender. Place sesame seed in a small, shallow baking pan and place in the oven for about the last 15 minutes, or until they are golden brown. Sprinkle the browned seed, salt, and pepper over the carrots before serving. Makes 6 servings.

## Fresh Orange Sundae

Spoon thawed frozen orange juice concentrate (or the orange juice and banana blend) over vanilla ice cream scoops. Pass sliced almonds to sprinkle on top.

# Meat Loaf with Sour Cream Topping

Part of the moisture of this meat loaf comes from eggplant, which is ground with the meat mixture. The yellow topping bakes to a custard consistency.

1 pound round steak
1 pound lean pork
2 medium-sized eggplants, peeled and quartered
1 medium-sized onion, peeled and halved
¼ cup finely chopped parsley
2 teaspoons salt
4 whole cloves
1 clove garlic
2 egg yolks
1 cup (½ pint) sour cream

Put meats, eggplant, and onion through food chopper, using medium blade. Turn ground mixture into frying pan; add parsley, salt, cloves, and garlic. Stirring frequently, simmer for 20 minutes, or until mixture is dry; remove garlic. Regrind mixture, using the fine blade of the food chopper. Pack ground mixture into a greased 6 by 9-inch baking pan. Beat egg yolks, combine with sour cream, then spread over top of the meat mixture. Bake in a moderately slow oven (325°) for 45 minutes. Cut into squares to serve. Makes 8 servings.

*Mexican casserole of beef, tomato, egg, cheese, seasonings is the main dish for the brunch on page 45. Casserole heats while guests enjoy cantaloupe wedges.*

# CASSEROLES

## *make-ahead favorites that cook themselves*

## Corn and Beef Bake

Red, green, and yellow vegetables make layers in this ground beef casserole dish.

¼ cup (4 tablespoons) shortening or salad oil
1 medium-sized onion, chopped
2 small green peppers, seeded and chopped
1 pound ground beef
2 teaspoons salt
¼ teaspoon pepper
2 eggs
1 can (1 lb.) whole kernel corn, drained
4 medium-sized tomatoes,
    cut in ¼-inch-thick slices
½ cup dry bread crumbs
2 tablespoons butter or margarine

Heat shortening in a large, heavy frying pan; add onion and green peppers and cook until onion is clear. Stir in ground beef and continue cooking until it is browned and crumbly; remove pan from heat and stir in salt and pepper. Beat eggs well, then stir quickly into meat mixture. Arrange half of the meat mixture in the bottom of a lightly greased 2-quart casserole; cover with half the drained corn, and top with half the tomato slices. Spoon in the remaining meat mixture, cover with the remaining corn, and top with the remaining tomato slices. Toss bread crumbs in melted butter, then sprinkle over top of casserole. Bake in a moderately hot oven (375°) for 30 minutes. Makes 6 servings.

## Macaroni Beef Casserole

You can make this dish ahead of time and reheat it, covered, in a slow oven (300°).

2 pounds ground beef
1 medium-sized onion, chopped
½ cup (¼ lb.) butter or margarine
1 package (8 oz.) macaroni, cooked and drained
¼ cup catsup
¼ cup bouillon, white wine, or water
1 cup shredded Cheddar cheese
⅓ cup chopped parsley
½ teaspoon pepper
½ teaspoon cinnamon
2 teaspoons salt
⅓ cup flour
2½ cups milk
1 teaspoon salt
1 teaspoon dry mustard
3 eggs, slightly beaten

Sauté ground beef and onion in 2 tablespoons of the butter until browned and crumbly. Combine with the cooked macaroni, catsup, bouillon, ½ cup of the cheese, parsley, pepper, cinnamon, and the 2 teaspoons salt. Turn into a greased 13 by 9 by 3 inch baking pan. Heat remaining 6 tablespoons butter, add flour and cook until bubbly. Gradually stir in milk. Add the 1 teaspoon salt and the mustard and cook, stirring, until thickened. Gradually stir the hot mixture into eggs. Pour into the casserole. Sprinkle with remaining ½ cup cheese. Bake in a moderate oven (350°) for about 30 minutes; let stand for about 15 minutes. Makes 8 to 10 servings.

## Spinach Fandango

This dish brings together an assortment of food flavors similar to those that are often found in Italian cookery.

1 pound lean ground chuck
1 medium-sized onion, chopped
1 can (6 or 8 oz.) mushrooms, drained
1 or 2 cloves garlic, chopped or pressed
1 teaspoon oregano
¼ cup salad oil, peanut oil, or olive oil
Salt and pepper to taste
2 packages (12 oz. each) frozen chopped spinach
1 can (10½ oz.) cream of celery soup
1 cup sour cream
2 large slices Mozzarella or jack cheese

In a large skillet or electric frying pan, combine ground beef, onion, mushrooms, garlic, and oregano and brown in the oil. Salt and pepper to taste. Place spinach unthawed on top of other ingredients, cover, and let steam until mixable. In a medium-sized casserole, mix semi-cooked ingredients with cream of celery soup and sour cream. Cut cheese in strips and garnish the top with them. Bake, uncovered, in a moderate oven (350°) for 15 to 20 minutes. Makes 4 servings.

## Beef Casserole, Chinese Style

In this ground beef casserole, the slices of crisp celery taste surprisingly like water chestnuts.

1 pound ground beef
1 package (10 oz.) frozen peas, thawed
2 cups finely sliced raw celery
1 can (10¾ oz.) mushroom soup
2 tablespoons light cream
¾ teaspoon salt
¼ teaspoon pepper
1 small onion, finely chopped
1 cup crushed potato chips

Cook ground beef in a frying pan until brown and crumbly, adding some fat if necessary; turn into a 1½-quart casserole. Arrange thawed peas over browned meat, then cover with the sliced celery. Mix together the mushroom soup, cream, salt, pepper, and onion; pour over celery. Sprinkle

potato chips over the top of the casserole. Bake in a moderately hot oven (375°) for 30 minutes, or until hot and bubbly. Makes 6 servings.

## Mexican Style Beef

If this is assembled and refrigerated, allow about 40 minutes to bake.

1 cup brown rice or regular rice
1 beef bouillon cube
1 medium-sized onion, thinly sliced
¼ cup butter, margarine, or salad oil
1 pound ground beef
1 clove garlic, minced or mashed
1 tablespoon chili powder
2 teaspoons dry mustard
1 teaspoon salt
1 can (1 lb.) tomatoes
1 can (1 lb.) kidney beans, drained
1 teaspoon paprika
¼ cup grated Parmesan cheese

Cook rice as directed on the package, except dissolve bouillon cube in the liquid called for in directions before stirring in the rice. Meanwhile in a frying pan sauté onion in butter until golden. Crumble in the ground beef; add garlic, chili powder, mustard, and salt. Cook, stirring, until meat loses its red color. Layer half of meat mixture in bottom of a 2-quart casserole. Spread cooked rice in a layer over meat. Spoon canned tomatoes over the rice, then spoon kidney beans over tomatoes. Layer remaining meat on top. Combine paprika with cheese, sprinkle over top. Bake, uncovered, in a moderate oven (350°) for about 30 minutes. Makes 6 servings.

## Noodles with Cheese-Meat Sauce

Several kinds of cheese, plus sour cream, insure a creamy richness in this 30-minute casserole.

1 package (8 oz.) wide egg noodles
Boiling salted water
1 pound ground beef
1 clove garlic, minced or mashed
½ teaspoon salt
2 cans (8 oz. each) Spanish style tomato sauce
1 small package (3 oz.) cream cheese
½ pint (1 cup) sour cream
3 tablespoons cottage cheese
6 green onions and tops, finely sliced
½ cup shredded Cheddar cheese

Cook noodles in boiling, salted water until tender; drain. Meanwhile, brown meat, stirring with a fork until crumbly; stir in garlic and salt. Add tomato sauce and simmer over low heat while noodles cook. Mix together the cream cheese, sour cream, cottage cheese, and green onions and tops. Alternate layers of noodles, meat sauce, and cream cheese mixture in a 2½-quart casserole. Sprinkle the top with cheese. Bake in a moderate oven (350°) for 20 minutes. Makes 6 servings.

## Spaghetti-Beef Casserole with Mixed Nuts

Mixed nuts lend a crunchy richness to this baked ground beef and mushroom casserole.

1 package (8 oz.) spaghetti
Boiling salted water
2 large onions, finely chopped
2 tablespoons butter or salad oil
2 pounds ground beef
2 teaspoons salt
½ teaspoon pepper
1 can (10½ oz.) tomato soup
1 soup can water
1 can (3 or 4 oz.) sliced or chopped mushrooms
1 package (8 oz.) processed Cheddar cheese, cut in pieces
1 teaspoon sugar
2 tablespoons Worcestershire
1 can (7 oz.) salted mixed nuts

Cook spaghetti in a large amount of boiling salted water until barely tender; drain. Using a heavy kettle with a tight fitting cover, saute onions in butter until browned. Add ground beef and brown until meat is crumbly. Season with salt and pepper. Stir in soup and water. Add mushrooms, ⅔ of the cheese, sugar, and Worcestershire. Mix in the spaghetti. Cover and simmer for 20 minutes. Turn into a greased casserole. Push nuts (coarsely chopped, if you wish) down into the mixture in the casserole, and sprinkle the remaining cheese on top. Bake in a moderate oven (350°) for 30 minutes. Makes 8 to 10 servings.

## Ground Beef-Cabbage Casserole

Though similar in flavor to cabbage rolls, this casserole is easier to make.

1 medium-sized onion, chopped
6 tablespoons butter or margarine
½ to 1 pound ground chuck
1 cup cooked rice
2 hard-cooked eggs, coarsely chopped
1 small cabbage (about 1¼ pounds)
2 tablespoons flour
2 cloves garlic, mashed
2 tablespoons catsup
1 cup canned tomatoes
1 cup water
1 can (3 or 4 oz.) chopped mushrooms
1 tablespoon chopped parsley
1½ teaspoons salt
¼ teaspoon pepper

Sauté onion in 2 tablespoons of the butter until soft. Add beef and rice; cook briskly for about 3 minutes, stirring. Stir in chopped eggs and turn into a shallow casserole, about 2½-quart size. Shred cabbage finely and arrange over meat mixture.

Melt remaining 4 tablespoons butter and blend in flour; cook until bubbly, then remove from heat and stir in garlic, catsup, tomatoes, water, mushrooms (including their liquid), parsley, salt, and pepper. Simmer together, stirring, for about 5 minutes. Pour over cabbage in casserole. Cover and bake in a moderate oven (350°) for about 30 minutes. Makes about 8 servings.

# Lasagne Napoli

You can assemble this casserole hours ahead — even the night before—and keep it in the refrigerator, ready to bake.

1 medium-sized onion, finely chopped
1 clove garlic, minced or mashed
2 tablespoons olive oil or salad oil
1 pound ground chuck
1 can (3 or 4 oz.) sliced mushrooms
1 can (8 oz.) tomato sauce
1 can (6 oz.) tomato paste
2 teaspoons salt
1 teaspoon oregano
¾ cup water
2 eggs
1 package (10 oz.) frozen chopped spinach, thawed
1 cup cream-style cottage cheese
⅓ cup grated Parmesan cheese
1 package (12 oz.) lasagne, cooked and drained
1 package (8 oz.) American cheese slices
    cut in strips

In a medium-sized frying pan lightly brown onion and garlic in 1 tablespoon of the oil; add ground chuck, and break apart; cook until brown. Blend in mushrooms (including mushroom liquid), tomato sauce, tomato paste, 1 teaspoon of the salt, oregano, and water; simmer for 15 minutes. Meanwhile, mix 1 of the eggs with the spinach, cottage cheese, Parmesan cheese, remaining 1 tablespoon oil, and 1 teaspoon salt. Beat the second egg slightly and toss with cooked lasagne. Pour half the meat sauce in an oblong baking pan (about 9 by 13 inches) and cover with a layer of half the lasagne. Spread all the spinach mixture over lasagne. Complete layers with remaining lasagne and meat sauce. Cover and bake in a moderate oven (350°) for 45 minutes. Remove cover and arrange strips of American cheese on top; bake 15 minutes longer. Serve hot. Makes 6 to 8 servings.

# Pastitsio

If you are planning a buffet dinner soon, consider this Greek casserole for the entrée. It's an especially good choice for a large group.

2 medium-sized onions, chopped
¼ cup (4 tablespoons) butter or margarine
2 pounds lean ground beef
Dash each cinnamon, cloves, and allspice
2 teaspoons salt
½ teaspoon pepper
½ cup water
2 tablespoons tomato paste
1 package (1 lb.) elbow macaroni
3 eggs, slightly beaten
1 teaspoon salt
¾ cup grated Parmesan cheese

*Cream sauce:*
6 tablespoons butter
¾ cup flour
1 quart milk
3 eggs, slightly beaten
1 teaspoon salt

Sauté onion in butter until golden. Add meat and cook, stirring, until well browned. Add cinnamon, cloves, allspice, the 2 teaspoons salt, and pepper. Stir in water and tomato paste; simmer for 5 minutes. Set aside.

For the macaroni filling, cook macaroni according to directions on the package. Mix with the 3 eggs and the 1 teaspoon salt. Set aside while making cream sauce (below).

Spoon half of the macaroni filling into a buttered 9 by 13-inch pan, and sprinkle with ¼ cup of the Parmesan cheese. Place all of the meat mixture on top. Pour remaining macaroni filling over meat, and sprinkle with another ¼ cup of the Parmesan cheese. Then pour all of the cream sauce over the macaroni; sprinkle top with remaining ¼ cup Parmesan cheese. Bake in a moderate oven (350°) for 45 minutes, or until thoroughly heated (if refrigerated, bake for 1 hour). Makes 10 servings.

*Cream sauce:*
Melt butter in a pan. Gradually stir in flour and cook, stirring, until blended and bubbly. Gradually stir in milk and cook, stirring, until sauce is smooth and thickened. Stir in eggs and salt until well blended.

## Mexican Breakfast Casserole  *(see suggested menu below)* ✳

3 medium-sized tomatoes
3 tablespoons butter
1 small onion, sliced
½ cup diced green pepper
½ clove garlic, mashed
½ pound lean ground beef
¼ pound lean pork sausage meat
2 tablespoons flour
½ teaspoon salt
½ teaspoon chili powder
Dash of pepper
6 eggs
¼ pound jack cheese

Peel and halve tomatoes and scoop out centers, discarding seeds and reserving pulp; set aside. In a frying pan, melt butter and add onion, green pepper, and garlic; cook until vegetables are limp. Add ground beef, pork sausage, and tomato pulp; cook over medium heat, stirring, for 10 minutes.

Combine flour, salt, chili powder, and pepper, and sprinkle over the meat mixture; mix in well. Cook 3 or 4 minutes longer or until thickened. Turn mixture into an 8 by 12-inch baking dish. Arrange tomato shells, rounded side down, on the meat mixture. Carefully crack eggs and place one in each tomato shell. Cut cheese into strips and cross two strips over each egg-filled tomato. Bake in a moderate oven (350°) for 20 to 25 minutes (remove from oven when eggs are just underdone). Makes 6 servings.

---

## ✳ Casserole Brunch for Six

Fresh Cantaloupe with Lime Wedges
Mexican Breakfast Casserole *(see recipe above)*
Raisin Bread     Butter
Orange Marmalade     Cinnamon Sugar     Coffee

The combination of beef, tomato, egg, cheese, and seasonings gives the Mexican Breakfast Casserole flavors reminiscent of the classic Mexican egg dish, *Huevos Rancheros*. Bring the casserole to the table hot and bubbling to serve after your guests have finished their cantaloupe.

---

## Tamale Casserole

Canned tamales and tomato sauce top this beef loaf mixture and give the dish a south-of-the-border flavor.

1 pound lean ground beef
1 small onion, minced
½ cup soft bread cubes
¼ cup milk
1 teaspoon salt
1 can (15½ oz.) tamales
1 can (8 oz.) tomato sauce
¼ teaspoon oregano
6 drops liquid hot-pepper seasoning

Mix well ground beef, onion, bread cubes, milk, and salt. Pat lightly into the bottom of a 1½-quart casserole. Remove parchment from tamales and cut tamales in thick slices. Place tamale slices on top of beef. Blend sauce from tamales with tomato sauce, oregano, and liquid hot-pepper seasoning. Pour over tamales. Bake in a moderately hot oven (375°) for 45 minutes. Makes 4 servings.

# Zucchini-Ground Beef Casserole

This casserole has a crusty, cheese-flavored topping. It's every bit as good when you prepare it a day ahead and reheat it just before serving.

1 pound ground beef
1 medium-sized onion, chopped
1 tablespoon salad oil
1 can (1 lb., 13 oz.) solid pack tomatoes
1 can (8 oz.) tomato sauce
1 can (6 oz.) tomato paste
1 small green pepper, seeded and chopped
¼ pound (1 cup) shredded sharp Cheddar cheese
6 medium-sized zucchini, sliced ½ inch thick
½ cup pitted ripe olives
½ teaspoon salt
Freshly ground pepper to taste
¼ teaspoon garlic salt
⅛ teaspoon oregano
Grated Parmesan cheese

Sauté meat and onion together in salad oil in a large frying pan until meat is browned and crumbly. Add tomatoes, tomato sauce, tomato paste, green pepper, Cheddar cheese, zucchini, and olives. Season with salt, pepper, garlic salt, and oregano. Simmer, uncovered, for 10 minutes. Turn into an 8 by 12-inch baking pan and sprinkle generously with the Parmesan cheese. Bake in a moderate oven (350°) for 1 hour, or until sauce is thickened and the top is nicely browned and slightly crusty. Makes 8 servings.

# Norwegian Meat Pudding

This looks and tastes like a tender and well-seasoned meat loaf.

1½ pounds finely ground beef
3 medium-sized potatoes, cooked and mashed, or 3 cups unseasoned mashed potatoes
2 tablespoons flour
1 small onion, minced
1 egg, slightly beaten
3 teaspoons salt
½ teaspoon pepper
½ teaspoon nutmeg
1 cup evaporated milk

Combine meat and potatoes. Add flour, minced onion, egg, salt, pepper, and nutmeg. Gradually work in undiluted evaporated milk, adding a tablespoon at a time. Blend thoroughly. Pour into well-greased 1½-quart deep casserole. Bake in a slow oven (300°) for 1½ hours, or until done. Test by inserting a sharp knife; if it comes out clean, the pudding is done. Cut into individual portions and separate to make them easy to lift out. Makes 6 to 8 servings.

# Western Meal-in-One

This is a good looking and delicious casserole to carry to a pot luck supper. If you wish to assemble it in the morning and refrigerate it, allow 1½ hours for baking.

1 pound ground beef
1 tablespoon salad oil or bacon drippings
1 clove garlic, minced or mashed
1 teaspoon salt
1 large onion, finely chopped
1 green pepper, seeded and chopped
1 teaspoon chili powder
1 can (1 lb.) tomatoes
1 can (1 lb.) kidney beans
¾ cup uncooked rice
¼ cup chopped ripe olives
¾ cup shredded Cheddar cheese

Brown the ground meat in oil until crumbly. Add garlic, salt, onion, green pepper, and chili powder, and sauté for 5 minutes, or until vegetables are limp. Mix in tomatoes, kidney beans, and rice, and turn into a greased 2-quart casserole. Bake, uncovered, in a moderate oven (350°) for 45 minutes. Sprinkle with olives and cheese, and continue baking for 15 minutes longer, or until cheese is melted. Makes 8 servings.

## Beef in Cabbage Bundles

Ground beef with brown rice, deftly seasoned with dill, is wrapped in cabbage leaves to make this hearty casserole dish.

½ cup uncooked brown rice
1 pound lean ground beef
⅓ cup butter or margarine
½ cup finely chopped onion
2 tablespoons chopped green pepper or parsley
½ teaspoon dill weed
1 teaspoon salt
¼ teaspoon pepper
8 large cabbage leaves, wilted,
   and with thick stem removed
Flour
2 cups liquid (half tomato juice and half bouillon,
   or ½ cup white wine and 1½ cups tomato juice
   or bouillon)
Sour cream

Cook rice according to directions on package. Lightly brown meat in 3 tablespoons of the butter; add onions and cook for 5 minutes. Stir in rice, green pepper or parsley, and seasonings. Divide meat filling among leaves and fold leaves, using envelope wrap, and roll to seal; tie or fasten with toothpicks. Flour rolls and brown in remaining butter; arrange in a casserole (about 2-quart size). Heat liquid (use same pan in which rolls were browned) and pour over rolls. Cover and bake in a moderate oven (350°) for 1 hour. Add a little water if rolls become dry. Serve rolls with pan juices and a dollop of sour cream. Makes 8 servings.

*Pineapple chunks add fruit flavor to casserole of beans topped with small meat balls (recipe below).*

## Pineapple Beans with Meat Balls

Pineapple chunks combine with canned kidney beans and pork and beans to give a tasty flavor to this casserole, which is attractively topped with meat balls.

1½ pounds ground beef
1 medium-sized onion, chopped
1 teaspoon salt
2 tablespoons salad oil
1 cup catsup
½ cup water
¼ cup brown sugar, firmly packed
2 tablespoons vinegar
2 teaspoons dry mustard
1 can (about 1 lb.) kidney beans, drained
2 cans (1 lb., 5 oz. each) pork and beans in tomato
   sauce
1 can (1 lb., 4 oz.) pineapple chunks, drained

Combine ground beef with the onion and salt. Form into small balls about 1½ inches in diameter. In a frying pan, brown the meat balls on all sides in the oil. Add catsup, water, brown sugar, vinegar, and mustard; stir until well blended. Bring mixture to a boil; reduce heat and simmer for 5 minutes.

In 2½-quart casserole, combine kidney beans, pork and beans, and pineapple, reserving ½ cup of the pineapple. Pour reserved pineapple, meat balls, and sauce over the beans. Bake uncovered in a moderately hot oven (375°) for 45 minutes. Makes 8 servings.

## Eggplant Lasagne *(see suggested menu below)* ✳

1 pound ground beef
2 medium-sized onions, chopped
1 teaspoon salt
½ teaspoon oregano
1 can (8 oz.) tomato sauce
1 package (10 oz.) frozen chopped spinach
1 large eggplant, cut in lengthwise slices ⅜ inch
   thick
Salt
2 eggs, beaten
About ¼ cup salad oil
¼ pound Mozzarella cheese, thinly sliced

Brown beef and onions in a frying pan. Stir in salt, oregano, and tomato sauce. Simmer for 10 minutes. Add frozen spinach and continue cooking until spinach is thawed. If necessary, skim fat from sauce.

While meat sauce is simmering, salt eggplant slices and dip in egg. In a frying pan heat enough oil to coat the bottom; brown eggplant slices on all sides, a few pieces at a time, adding oil as needed. Make a layer of ⅓ of the eggplant slices in bottom of a deep 2-quart casserole. Spoon in ⅓ of the meat sauce; top with two more alternating layers of eggplant and sauce, finishing with the sauce. Cover surface with sliced cheese. At this point you can cover the casserole and refrigerate it until ready to bake. Bake in a moderately hot oven (375°) for 30 minutes. Makes 6 servings.

---

## ✳ Supper to Make in the Morning

Eggplant Lasagne *(see recipe above)*
Tossed Salad          Hot French Bread
Chilled Crenshaw Melon with Lime

When you serve this casserole supper, you can handle all of the preparation and clean-up in the morning. The only thing you'll have to do before the evening meal is to make the salad: use an assortment of crisp raw vegetables and greens and toss with your favorite dressing. Heat a sliced and buttered loaf of French bread in the oven while the casserole bakes.

---

## Ground Beef and Hominy Bake

This combination of well-seasoned beef and hominy grits needs no attention during the baking period. It comes from the oven moist and flavorful, topped with a layer of melted cheese.

1 pound ground beef
1 medium-sized onion, finely chopped
1 green pepper, finely chopped
½ teaspoon salt
½ to 1 teaspoon chili powder
1 cup cooked hominy grits
½ cup bouillon
1 can (8 oz.) tomato sauce
½ cup shredded Cheddar cheese
½ cup fine dry bread crumbs

Brown ground beef with onion and green pepper until meat is crumbly, adding a little fat if necessary. Season meat mixture with salt and chili powder to taste. Combine with hominy grits, bouillon, and tomato sauce; then mix thoroughly. Spoon into a lightly greased 2-quart casserole, sprinkle with cheese, cover with bread crumbs. Bake in a moderate oven (350°) for 30 minutes. Makes 6 servings.

## Baked Beans with Ground Beef Topping

You can serve this casserole either as a main dish or as an especially hearty side dish.

1 pound ground beef
¼ cup chopped green pepper
½ cup finely chopped onion
½ cup sliced celery
1 can (8 oz.) tomato sauce
½ cup water
2 tablespoons vinegar
1 clove garlic, minced or mashed
1 teaspoon dry mustard
½ teaspoon thyme
1 tablespoon brown sugar
Salt and pepper
1 can (1 lb., 12 oz.) pork and beans

In a large frying pan, cook ground beef in its own fat; add green pepper, onion, and celery, and sauté until beef is brown and vegetables are limp. Stir in tomato sauce, water, vinegar, garlic, mustard, thyme, brown sugar, and salt and pepper to taste. Simmer together for 5 minutes. Turn pork and beans into a greased 1½-quart baking dish; spoon meat mixture over the top. Bake in a moderately hot oven (375°) for 45 minutes. Makes 6 servings as a main dish, 8 as a side dish.

## Spinach Tortina

You might make a rich tomato sauce to ladle, hot, over squares of this hearty tortina. Or use canned tomato sauce and heat thoroughly. Then sprinkle with Parmesan cheese.

1 pound ground beef
1 pound fresh spinach
1 small onion, chopped
Boiling salted water
2 eggs, beaten
1 tablespoon grated Parmesan cheese
1½ teaspoons salt
½ teaspoon pepper
2 tablespoons butter or margarine
Additional Parmesan cheese

Slowly brown ground beef; drain off excess fat; set aside. Trim stems from spinach; wash and rinse the leaves; chop coarsely. Cook spinach and onion in boiling salted water for 3 to 5 minutes or until tender; drain. Combine ground beef, spinach, onions, eggs, Parmesan cheese, salt, and pepper. In a moderate oven (350°), melt butter in a 1½-quart baking dish. Turn meat and spinach mixture into heated baking dish. Return to oven and bake for 30 minutes, or until set. Serve with additional Parmesan cheese. Makes 4 servings.

## Ground Beef Casserole, Deluxe

A generous proportion of cottage cheese combined with cream cheese makes this an unusual beef casserole. You can prepare it ahead of time and refrigerate it, but bake it just before serving as it doesn't reheat well.

1 package (8 oz.) noodles
1 pound ground beef
1 tablespoon shortening or salad oil
2 cans (8 oz. each) tomato sauce
1 pint (2 cups) cottage cheese
1 large package (8 oz.) cream cheese
¼ cup sour cream
⅓ cup chopped green onions, including some of the tops
1 tablespoon finely chopped green pepper

Cook the noodles in boiling salted water until nearly tender, about 9 minutes; drain. In a large frying pan, brown the ground beef in the shortening, crumbling it with a fork. Add tomato sauce and remove from heat. Combine the cottage cheese, cream cheese, sour cream, green onions, and green pepper; mix well. Spread half of the noodles in a greased 2-quart casserole. Cover with the cheese mixture. Spread the remaining noodles over cheese. Top with the ground beef mixture. Bake uncovered in a moderate oven (350°) for about 30 minutes, until bubbly. Makes 6 to 8 servings.

# Hominy Tamale Pie

This meaty tamale pie differs from the cornmeal version: a crust of hominy covers the colorful filling. You can make it a day in advance and reheat it just before serving time.

1 can (1 lb., 12 oz.) white or yellow hominy
1 egg
2 tablespoons melted shortening or salad oil
¾ pound ground beef
½ pound bulk pork sausage
1 medium-sized onion, chopped
1 tablespoon brown sugar
1 tablespoon chili powder
1 teaspoon garlic salt
½ teaspoon cumin seed or
    ¼ teaspoon cumin powder
1 can (3 or 4 oz.) chopped or sliced olives, drained
1 can (8 oz.) tomato sauce
½ cup shredded Cheddar cheese
¼ cup shredded or grated Parmesan cheese

Thoroughly drain the hominy; save ½ cup of the liquid. Reserve about ¾ cup of hominy, and put the remainder through a food chopper or electric blender. Mix the ground hominy with the reserved hominy liquid; stir in the egg and melted shortening. Line the bottom and sides of a greased, 2-quart shallow casserole with hominy mixture; set aside.

Crumble the ground beef and the pork sausage into a frying pan; begin cooking. When meat is about half done, add chopped onion; cook until meat is browned and onions are transparent. Drain off the excess fat. Stir in the sugar, chili powder, garlic salt, and cumin seed; cook for about 5 minutes over medium heat. Add olives, tomato sauce, and the remaining whole hominy. Heat through and pour into the lined casserole. Top with the shredded Cheddar cheese, then with Parmesan cheese. Bake in a moderate oven (350°) for 30 minutes. Makes 6 servings.

# Corn Chip Chili

3 cans (15 oz. each) red kidney beans, drained
2 cans (about 10 oz. each) enchilada sauce
2 cups shredded Cheddar cheese
1½ tablespoons chili powder
1 package (6 oz.) corn chips
1½ pounds ground chuck
1½ cups chopped onions
1 clove garlic, minced
2 tablespoons salad oil or olive oil
1 cup (approximately) sour cream

Combine kidney beans, enchilada sauce, Cheddar cheese, chili powder, and corn chips. Sauté ground chuck, onions, and garlic in oil until meat is brown and onions are tender. Stir together meat and bean mixtures; pour into a 3-quart baking dish, and bake in a moderate oven (350°) for about 30 minutes, until hot and bubbly. Remove from oven, top with dollops of sour cream. Return to oven, and heat for 5 minutes longer. Makes 8 to 10 servings.

# Garbanzo Bean Casserole

This casserole is made with canned garbanzos and sliced water chestnuts, with a sprinkling of Cheddar cheese added before it goes into the oven.

1½ pounds ground beef
1 teaspoon salt
½ teaspoon pepper
½ teaspoon garlic salt
2 large onions, chopped
1 can (about 1 lb., 13 oz.) tomatoes
2 cans (about 1 lb. each) garbanzo beans, drained
1 can (about 5 oz.) water chestnuts,
  drained and sliced
½ cup shredded sharp Cheddar cheese

In a large frying pan (one that has a cover), brown the meat; add the salt, pepper, garlic salt, and onions. Add tomatoes, cover, and simmer for 30 minutes. Add the beans and chestnuts to meat mixture and stir until well blended. Pour into a 2½-quart casserole. Sprinkle the cheese on top, and bake, uncovered, in a moderate oven (350°) for about 30 minutes, or until lightly browned. Makes 6 to 8 servings.

## Spanish Rice with Beef

For this spicy casserole, you brown uncooked rice, add beef and sauces, and cook all together in an electric frying pan.

1½ tablespoons bacon drippings
1¼ cups uncooked rice
1 medium-sized onion, finely chopped
1 clove garlic, minced or mashed
1 pound ground beef
1 can (1 lb.) tomatoes
1 can (6 oz.) mushroom sauce
1 can (8 oz.) tomato sauce
1 can (3 or 4 oz.) mushroom stems and pieces
¼ teaspoon oregano
¼ teaspoon chili powder
¼ teaspoon pepper
1 teaspoon salt

Heat bacon drippings in electric frying pan at 300° and sauté rice, onion, and garlic until golden. Add meat and cook, stirring, until the meat is browned and crumbly. Add tomatoes, mushroom sauce, tomato sauce, mushrooms and liquid, oregano, chili powder, pepper, and salt; mix well. Cover and simmer at 250° for 1 hour. Makes 6 servings.

## Spaghetti Meat Loaf Casserole

Traditional spaghetti sauce seasonings are used in this casserole, a good family main dish. Serve it with a tossed salad, garlic bread, and a fruit dessert.

1 egg
¾ cup tomato juice
1 teaspoon salt
¼ teaspoon pepper
¼ teaspoon garlic salt
¼ teaspoon oregano
¼ teaspoon rosemary
1 teaspoon Worcestershire
½ cup soft bread crumbs
1 small onion, chopped
1 can (15½ oz.) spaghetti in tomato sauce
1½ pounds ground beef
¼ pound sharp Cheddar cheese,
   cut into ½-inch cubes

In a large bowl, beat egg lightly with a fork. Add tomato juice, salt, pepper, garlic salt, oregano, rosemary, Worcestershire, bread crumbs, chopped onion, canned spaghetti, and ground beef. Mix together until well blended. Carefully mix in cheese cubes. Pack in a greased 2-quart casserole. Bake in a moderate oven (350°) for about 1 hour. Serve hot or cold. Makes 6 servings.

## Hamburger Fingerlings

This hamburger-sausage casserole assembles easily and can be reheated. The recipe can easily be doubled.

1 pound ground beef
½ pound pork sausage meat
1 can (10½ oz.) chicken and rice soup
2 eggs, slightly beaten
1 medium-sized onion, chopped
1 cup soft bread crumbs
½ teaspoon salt
⅛ teaspoon pepper
⅛ teaspoon garlic salt
¼ teaspoon poultry seasoning
Pinch of sweet basil
About 1 cup crushed cornflakes
2 tablespoons shortening or salad oil
1 can (10½ oz.) mushroom soup
   mixed with ½ soup can water

Combine ground beef with sausage meat, chicken and rice soup, eggs, onion, bread crumbs, salt, pepper, garlic salt, poultry seasoning, and basil. When well blended, shape into finger shapes about 1½ by 4 inches. Roll in the cornflake crumbs and brown on all sides in the shortening or oil. Place in a 9 by 13-inch baking dish. Pour over the mushroom soup mixed with water. Bake uncovered in a slow oven (300°) for about 1 hour. Makes 4 to 6 servings.

*Fresh cabbage soup with buttered croutons and an open-faced cheeseburger are complemented by green onion and diagonal slices of carrot in this hot lunch (page 55).*

52   QUICK ENTREES

# QUICK ENTRÉES

## *simple and delicious, based on ground beef*

### *Avocado Ground Beef*

Avocado enriches and colors the tangy yogurt sauce.

1½ pounds ground beef
1 medium-sized onion, chopped
½ teaspoon salt
½ teaspoon garlic salt
1 teaspoon pepper
1 can (10½ oz.) cream of mushroom soup
1 cup yogurt
1 medium-sized avocado, cubed
3 cups hot steamed rice

Lightly brown ground beef in its own juices. Add onion, salt, garlic salt, and pepper. Cook slowly, covered, about 30 minutes. Blend in soup, and cook for 5 minutes more. (Add a little water if the mixture seems too thick.) Fold in yogurt and avocado. Cook just until heated through. Serve immediately with rice. Makes 4 to 6 servings.

### *Quick Hamburger Hash*

Soy sauce gives this dish its fresh, zesty flavor.

3 tablespoons bacon fat or salad oil
1 pound ground chuck
½ medium-sized onion, chopped
¼ teaspoon salt
Dash of pepper
½ cup soy sauce
2 cups shredded raw potato

Heat fat in a large frying pan. Crumble in the ground meat; add onions, and brown until onions are golden. Stir in salt, pepper, and soy sauce. Mound potatoes over meat, cover pan, turn heat to medium low, and cook for 20 to 25 minutes,

stirring occasionally from the bottom.

You can serve the hash at this point—the potatoes will be done, but not crisp. If you prefer crisp potatoes, remove the cover after 20 minutes of cooking and continue to cook, stirring, until the potatoes brown slightly on all sides. Makes 4 servings.

### *Tropical Beef on Crisp Noodles*

Skillet-toasted coconut and ground beef are combined with a pineapple juice sauce for a sweet-sour entrée to serve over crisp noodles.

1 cup flaked coconut
1 pound ground beef
1 teaspoon salt
¼ teaspoon nutmeg
1¼ cups pineapple juice
2 teaspoons lemon juice
2 tablespoons cornstarch
½ cup water
1 can (about 6 oz.) chow mein noodles
3 tablespoons salted almonds

Toss coconut in a heated frying pan until brown and crisp; remove and set aside. In the same frying pan, brown ground beef slightly, adding a small amount of oil if needed. Add salt, nutmeg, and coconut. Combine pineapple juice and lemon juice, and add to beef mixture. Mix cornstarch and water until smooth. Stir into beef mixture; heat and stir for about 5 minutes or until liquid is thickened and all ingredients are coated with sauce. Arrange fried noodles on a platter and top with coconut-beef mixture. Garnish with a sprinkling of salted almonds. Makes 4 servings.

## Ground Beef and Rice Medley

Meat, vegetables, and rice are combined here for a colorful entrée.

2 medium-sized onions
3 medium-sized carrots
2 stalks celery
1 green pepper, seeded
1 pound ground beef
2 tablespoons shortening or salad oil
1 teaspoon salt
½ teaspoon pepper
2 bouillon cubes
2½ cups hot water
1 cup uncooked rice

Put the onions, carrots, celery, and green pepper through the medium blade of a food chopper. In a heavy kettle with a tight-fitting cover, brown meat in melted shortening until crumbly; season with salt and pepper. Dissolve bouillon cubes in the hot water. Stir chopped vegetables, bouillon, and rice into the meat mixture. Cover and simmer slowly for 45 minutes, or until rice is fluffy. Makes 6 servings.

## Cheese and Beef Open-Faced Sandwich

Slice open a loaf of French bread, layer the cut surface with one ingredient after another, bake briefly, and you have a hearty open-faced sandwich. Cut it into fat strips to serve. Use amount of seasoning ingredients that suit your own tastes, but be sure to spread ingredients well to the edges of the bread so all cut surfaces are covered.

1 small loaf French bread
Soft butter
Prepared mustard
Catsup
About 2 cloves garlic, finely minced
½ pound very sharp Cheddar cheese, thinly sliced
½ pound ground beef
Seasoned salt

Cut bread loaf in half lengthwise. Spread cut surfaces with soft butter. Smooth on prepared mustard, then catsup. Sprinkle minced garlic over surfaces. Arrange cheese slices, then the ground beef. Sprinkle with seasoned salt. Place on a baking sheet and bake in a moderate oven (350°) for 15 minutes or until cheese melts and beef browns. Cut crosswise into strips about 1½ inches wide. Serve immediately while very hot. Makes 4 generous servings as a supper entrée, about 8 servings as a snack.

## Beef and Vegetables in Sour Cream

This is a cross between Beef Stroganoff and Hungarian Paprika, with sour cream and paprika as its distinguishing seasoning ingredients. Carrot rings add color to the tangy sauce.

1 pound ground beef
1 large onion, chopped
¼ small green pepper, chopped
2 large carrots, thinly sliced
1 small can (2 or 3 oz.) mushrooms
1 clove garlic, minced or mashed
2 tablespoons salad oil or olive oil
¾ teaspoon salt
¼ teaspoon pepper
2 teaspoons paprika
⅓ cup water
¾ cup sour cream
Hot cooked broad noodles

Brown meat until crumbly, and set aside. In the same pan, sauté the onion, green pepper, carrots, drained mushrooms (reserve liquid), and garlic in the oil until onion is golden brown. Add browned meat, salt, pepper, paprika, mushroom liquid, and water; cover and simmer slowly for 30 minutes. Stir in the sour cream, and reheat, but do not boil. Serve over hot noodles. Makes 4 generous servings.

## Open-Faced Cheeseburgers  (*see suggested menu below*) ✳

1 small white onion, thinly sliced
1 tablespoon salad oil
1 pound lean ground beef
½ teaspoon salt
¼ teaspoon seasoned pepper
1 package (8 oz.) Mozzarella cheese
4 English muffins or hamburger buns
Prepared mustard
Catsup

Sauté onion slices in oil until translucent. Crumble in the ground beef and add salt and seasoned pepper; brown. Slice cheese in ¼-inch slices and cut each slice in 4 strips; reserve. Split muffins and spread each half lightly with mustard. Carefully spoon meat mixture on each half, cover with 3 or 4 strips of cheese, and top with about 1 teaspoon of catsup. Place on a baking sheet and broil about 6 inches below the heat until cheese is melted, about 3 minutes. Serve immediately. Makes 4 servings of 2 halves each.

---

## ✳ Soup and Burger Lunch

Cabbage Cream Soup
Open-Faced Cheeseburgers (*see recipe above*)
Vegetable Sticks
Cookies

This simple lunch menu is based on a fresh cabbage soup and a cheeseburger with a new twist to its preparation. Crisp vegetable sticks are a refreshing addition to the menu. Start the soup shortly before serving, or make it in advance and reheat. Assemble the open-faced burgers and broil just before serving. Prepare the vegetable sticks from carrots, celery, green onions, or cauliflower. Buy or make the cookies to serve as dessert.

### Cabbage Cream Soup

1 chicken bouillon cube
1 cup boiling water
3 cups shredded cabbage
2 tablespoons instant minced onion
2 tablespoons minced parsley
½ teaspoon thyme
½ teaspoon salt
1 tablespoon butter
1 cup canned or whole fresh milk
Buttered croutons

In a saucepan dissolve bouillon cube in boiling water. Bring to a boil, and add cabbage, onion, parsley, thyme, and salt. Cook for about 7 minutes. Pour into blender and whirl until smooth (or rub through a wire strainer); return to saucepan. Stir in butter and milk. Reheat just before serving. Garnish servings with buttered croutons. Makes 4 to 6 servings.

## Ground Beef Burgundy  *(see suggested menu below)* ✻

1 pound lean ground beef
Shortening
1 tablespoon flour
1 cup Burgundy
2 tablespoons dry onion soup mix
1 can (3 or 4 oz.) sliced mushrooms with liquid
¼ teaspoon dried thyme
¼ bay leaf
1 clove garlic, minced or mashed
1 tablespoon chopped fresh parsley
Hot cooked hominy, rice, or noodles

In a large frying pan, brown the beef in a small amount of shortening. Add flour; stir into meat and brown slightly. Add wine, onion soup mix, mushrooms and liquid, thyme, bay leaf, and garlic. Simmer for about 5 minutes, or until liquid is slightly reduced, stirring occasionally. Turn into a serving dish; sprinkle with the chopped parsley. Serve over hot golden hominy, rice, or noodles. Makes 4 servings.

## ✻ Make-ahead Family Supper

Ground Beef Burgundy *(see recipe above)*
Golden Hominy or Hot Steamed Rice or Buttered Noodles
Crisp Cucumber-Green Pepper Salad
Strawberry-Pineapple Fruit Cup
Toasted Coconut Pudding Sauce

When the supper hour is uncertain, you can prepare all of this meal ahead of time. At serving time, simply reheat the main dish, arrange the salad platter, and take the dessert out of the refrigerator.

### Crisp Cucumber-Green Pepper Salad

2 large cucumbers
2 teaspoons salt
½ green pepper
Salt
Lettuce
1 medium-sized tomato, thinly sliced
2 tablespoons vinegar
2 tablespoons water
2 teaspoons sugar
Dash of pepper

Peel cucumbers and grate or slice very thin. Sprinkle with the 2 teaspoons salt; mix thoroughly. Chill for at least 1 hour. Slice green pepper into thin slivers; sprinkle lightly with salt. Chill. At serving time, line a shallow bowl with crisp torn lettuce. With your hands, squeeze excess liquid from cucumbers. Shape them in a mound in center of lettuce. Squeeze green peppers in the same way, and arrange them in a border around cucumber mound. Garnish salad with tomato slices. Pour over a dressing made by stirring together the vinegar, water, sugar, and pepper. Makes 4 servings.

### Strawberry-Pineapple Fruit Cup

1 cup cubed fresh pineapple
1 cup sliced strawberries
1 package (3½ oz.) toasted coconut pudding
2¾ cups milk

Divide pineapple cubes and strawberries among 4 fruit bowls. Chill. Make toasted coconut pudding according to directions on package, except use 2¾ cups milk. At serving time, pass pudding as a sauce to ladle over fruits. Makes 4 servings.

# Gumbo Ground Beef

Crumbled ground beef plus a can of soup makes this successful quick dish.

1 pound ground beef
½ cup chopped onion
¾ teaspoon salt
¼ teaspoon pepper
1 can (10½ oz.) chicken gumbo soup
2 tablespoons catsup
2 tablespoons prepared mustard
Hot cooked rice, mashed potatoes, or
   split toasted hamburger buns

Brown meat and onion together until meat is crumbly, adding a little fat, if necessary. Season with salt and pepper, and stir in soup, catsup, and mustard. Simmer over low heat for 30 minutes. Spoon over rice, potatoes, or toasted buns. Makes 6 servings.

# Chili Bean Taco

Here is one of the simplest ways to dress up chili con carne. Corn chips form the base; beans and shredded cheese are layered on top; and the result tastes like taco.

½ pound ground beef
1 small onion, chopped
1 can (about 1 lb.) chili con carne with beans
1 package (3¾ oz.) corn chips
Shredded sharp Cheddar cheese (about ¾ cup)
About 1 cup shredded lettuce
Prepared taco sauce

In a frying pan, brown the beef and onion. Stir in the beans; cover and simmer for 15 minutes. Arrange corn chips on a platter. Spread bean mixture over the chips. Sprinkle cheese over the beans. Pass the shredded lettuce and taco sauce at the table. Makes 4 servings.

# Ground Beef Curry

Here is a "last-minute" ground beef dish with a savory Middle East flavor. Parsley and pine nuts lend distinction to the curried sauce. For company fare, serve this with such condiments as sliced green onions, crisp bacon, and raisins plumped in wine.

1 medium-sized onion, chopped
1 tablespoon salad oil
1 pound ground beef
1 package (1¾ oz.) pine nuts
Salt and pepper to taste
1 teaspoon curry powder
¼ teaspoon garlic salt
2 cans (8 oz. each) tomato sauce
2 cups water
Juice of 2 lemons
1 bunch parsley, finely chopped
Hot steamed rice or cracked wheat pilaff

In a large frying pan, sauté onion in oil until golden. Add ground beef, pine nuts, salt and pepper to taste, curry powder, and garlic salt. Cook until meat is browned, stirring with a fork to keep it crumbly. Pour in tomato sauce and water. Cover and simmer for 10 minutes to let the flavors mingle. Add lemon juice and simmer for 5 minutes longer. Just before serving, stir in chopped parsley and cook just until heated through. Serve over steamed rice or cracked wheat pilaff. Makes 4 servings.

## Beef-Bacon Rolls

*(see suggested menu opposite)* *

8 slices bacon
4 tablespoons fresh bread crumbs
1 tablespoon minced parsley
1 pound ground beef
1 teaspoon instant minced onion
½ teaspoon seasoned pepper
½ teaspoon salt
¼ teaspoon monosodium glutamate

Fry 4 slices of the bacon until crisp; drain and mince. Brown bread crumbs in about 2 tablespoons of the bacon drippings. Combine parsley with bread crumbs and minced bacon; reserve. Season ground beef with instant minced onion, seasoned pepper, salt, and monosodium glutamate.

On a board, pat meat mixture out to form a 10-inch square; quarter to get 4 smaller squares. Place a line of bacon-crumb filling down the center of each square; bring together the meat edges that run parallel to the filling and gently shape into a roll. Wrap a strip of uncooked bacon around each meat roll and fasten with a toothpick. Brown on all sides in a lightly oiled frying pan. Arrange with Mashed Potatoes Parmesan (see recipe below) in a shallow baking dish, and bake in a moderate oven (350°) for 15 to 20 minutes. (If you make this in advance and refrigerate it, allow a longer baking time.) Makes 4 servings.

## Avocado with Chili con Carne

In this recipe, the contrast is the thing—spicy, robust chili con carne, heaped on the mild and mellow avocado.

1 medium-sized onion, chopped
1 clove garlic, minced or mashed
3 to 4 tablespoons butter or salad oil
½ to ¾ pound lean ground beef
1 can (1 lb.) tomatoes
1½ teaspoons salt
3 teaspoons chili powder, or to taste
1 can (1 lb.) red kidney beans, undrained
3 avocados

Cook onion and garlic slowly in the butter or oil until soft. Add beef and cook until lightly

*Meat Rolls, Mashed Potatoes Parmesan, Mincemeat Apples bake together for the oven dinner opposite.*

browned. Add tomatoes, salt, chili powder, and beans; stir to blend. Simmer for about 15 minutes. Spoon hot chili over peeled, room-temperature avocado halves, and serve immediately. Makes 6 servings.

## Beef and Cheese Pie

The base of this entrée is ground beef, and the trimmings are those that give pizza its distinctive flavor.

1 pound ground beef
⅔ cup evaporated milk
¼ cup fine dry bread crumbs
1 teaspoon garlic salt
⅓ cup catsup
1 can (2 or 3 oz.) sliced mushrooms, drained
1 cup (¼ lb.) shredded Cheddar cheese
¼ teaspoon crumbled oregano
2 tablespoons grated Parmesan cheese

Combine meat, milk, bread crumbs, and garlic salt in a 9-inch pie pan; pat mixture against sides and bottom of pie pan. Spread catsup over the meat mixture; sprinkle with mushrooms, Cheddar cheese, oregano, and Parmesan cheese. Bake in a very hot oven (450°) for 20 minutes or until meat is done to your taste. Cut into wedges to serve. Makes 4 servings.

# *Oven Dinner for a Busy Day

Beef-Bacon Rolls (*see recipe opposite*)
Green Bean Salad
Mashed Potatoes Parmesan
Baked Mincemeat Apples

Make this meal in less than an hour from start to service, or make it in advance and put it in the oven about 20 minutes before serving. Cook the beans for the salad and chill. The other three dishes go into the oven together, so make each up to the baking point, then bake or refrigerate.

### Green Bean Salad

2 packages (9 oz. each) frozen cut green beans
¼ cup salad oil
¼ cup wine vinegar
½ teaspoon salt
¼ teaspoon garlic salt
¼ teaspoon pepper
2 tablespoons finely sliced canned pimiento
Lettuce

Cook beans as directed on package; cool. Make dressing by combining salad oil and vinegar; stir in salt, garlic salt, pepper, and pimiento. Shortly before serving, spoon cooled beans into a lettuce-lined bowl, pour dressing over the top; chill until serving time. Makes 4 to 5 servings.

### Mashed Potatoes Parmesan

Mash and season potatoes for 4 servings (or use instant mashed potato mix). Place in the center of a shallow baking dish; smooth top. Pour 2 tablespoons melted butter evenly over the top; sprinkle with 1½ tablespoons shredded Parmesan cheese. Bake (with Beef-Bacon Rolls, above) for 15 to 20 minutes in a moderate oven (350°). Makes 4 servings.

### Baked Mincemeat Apples

½ cup prepared mincemeat
3 tablespoons orange juice
¼ teaspoon freshly grated orange peel
4 cooking apples, cored but not peeled

Combine mincemeat, orange juice, and orange peel. Spoon mixture into the centers of the apples. Place apples in buttered individual custard cups and bake uncovered in a moderate oven (350°) for 45 minutes. (Put them in with the meat and potatoes, but cook ½ hour longer.) Makes 4 servings.

## Beef-Stuffed Green Peppers

Ground beef makes a simple and delicious stuffing for bell peppers.

8 to 10 green bell peppers
Boiling salted water
1½ pounds ground beef
2 medium-sized onions, chopped
1½ cups cooked rice
¼ cup grated Parmesan cheese
1 egg
1½ teaspoons salt
½ teaspoon pepper

Slice off top (stem) end of peppers; remove seeds and veins. Drop peppers into boiling salted water, and boil for 5 minutes; drain. Brown beef in a frying pan. Add onions, and cook until wilted. Mix with rice, cheese, egg, salt, and pepper. Fill prepared pepper shells, arrange in a baking pan and bake in a moderate oven (350°) for about 20 minutes or until tender. Makes 8 to 10 servings.

# SOME SPECIAL ENTRÉES

## *serve these to guests*

## *Beef and Onion Tostadas*

Crisp-fried tortillas form the base of these Mexican-style open-faced sandwiches. One tostada is a whole meal for one person for lunch or supper.

1 large sweet onion
French dressing
1 small onion, chopped
1 pound ground beef
1 tablespoon shortening
1 can (8 oz.) tomato sauce
2 teaspoons Worcestershire
½ teaspoon oregano
½ teaspoon cumin
Dash of pepper
Dash of liquid hot-pepper seasoning
4 tortillas
Salad oil or shortening
1 cup shredded sharp Cheddar cheese
4 slices tomato
4 slices cucumber
Canned green chili sauce

Peel and thinly slice the sweet onion; dress with French dressing and chill for several hours. Sauté chopped onion and beef in the 1 tablespoon shortening until browned. Add tomato sauce, Worcestershire, oregano, cumin, pepper, and hot-pepper seasoning; cook, stirring, for about 5 minutes.

Heat 1 inch of salad oil or shortening in a frying pan, and fry 1 tortilla at a time, using a spatula to hold it under the fat; it crisps and browns in about 2 minutes. Spread hot meat mixture on the crisp-fried tortillas; sprinkle with cheese, and top with the sliced onion, tomato, and cucumber. Serve with canned green chili sauce. Makes 4 servings.

## *Ham - Beef Rolls with Fruit*

Serve this festive looking and easy-to-make meat dish to family or guests.

¾ pound ground chuck
½ cup evaporated milk (or cream)
¼ cup dry bread crumbs
¼ cup chopped onion
½ teaspoon salt
Dash pepper
3 large thin slices ham
Whole cloves
2 tablespoons butter or margarine
½ cup brown sugar, firmly packed
2 tablespoons cornstarch
2 teaspoons prepared mustard
⅓ cup orange juice
About 1 cup fruit (fresh or canned apricots, pineapple, peaches, grapes, or cantaloupe)

Mix ground chuck lightly with evaporated milk, bread crumbs, onion, salt, and pepper. Spoon one-third of the mixture on each ham slice. Roll ham around meat; stud with cloves. Arrange with seam sides down in a shallow baking pan (about 9 by 12 inches). Melt butter; blend in brown sugar, cornstarch, mustard, and orange juice. Pour over the meat rolls. Bake, uncovered, in a moderate oven (350°) for about 30 minutes, basting several times with sauce in pan. Stir fruit into sauce in pan; bake for 15 minutes more. Cut rolls in half. Makes 6 servings.

---

*Jamaican Meat-stuffed Pumpkin (page 62) is an impressive main dish for a buffet or informal supper.*

*The ground beef filling is flavored with smoked ham, onion, green pepper, raisins, olives, capers, seasonings.*

# Jamaican Meat-Stuffed Pumpkin *(see suggested menu opposite)* ✳

1 small whole pumpkin or Hubbard squash,
    8 to 10 inches in diameter
Boiling salted water
2 tablespoons salad oil
2 pounds ground chuck
6 ounces ground smoked ham
2½ cups finely chopped onions
1 green pepper, finely chopped
2½ teaspoons salt
2 teaspoons olive oil
2 teaspoons oregano
1 teaspoon vinegar
1 teaspoon ground black pepper
Dash crushed dried red pepper
2 large cloves garlic, mashed
¾ cup raisins
⅓ cup pimiento-stuffed green olives, chopped
2 teaspoons capers, drained and minced
1 can (8 oz.) tomato sauce
3 eggs, beaten

With a sharp knife, cut a circular top (about 5 inches in diameter) out of the pumpkin. Save this top for the lid. Scoop out seeds, and scrape inside of pumpkin clean. Place pumpkin in a large pan and cover with salted water; cover pan. Bring water to a boil, then simmer until pumpkin meat is almost tender when pierced with a fork, about 30 minutes (the pumpkin should still be firm enough to hold its shape well). Carefully remove pumpkin from hot water, drain well, and dry the outside. Sprinkle inside with a little salt.

Heat salad oil in a large frying pan. Add beef, ham, onions, and green pepper. Cook over high heat, stirring, just until the meat is browned and crumbly. Remove meat from heat. Mix together salt, olive oil, oregano, vinegar, black pepper, red pepper, and garlic. Add to meat along with raisins, olives, capers, and tomato sauce. Mix well. Cover pan and cook over low heat for 15 minutes, stirring occasionally. Remove from heat and allow to cool slightly; then mix in the eggs thoroughly.

Fill cooked pumpkin with the meat stuffing, pressing the stuffing slightly to pack it firmly. Cover loosely with the pumpkin lid. Place pumpkin in a shallow greased baking pan and bake in a moderate oven (350°) for 1 hour. Allow to cool for 10 to 15 minutes before serving.

At serving time, carefully lift the meat-filled pumpkin (support the bottom with a wide spatula) to a serving plate or carving board; garnish with clean fall leaves or flowers, if desired. To serve, slice pumpkin from top to bottom in fat wedges. Lift each serving onto a dinner plate, and spoon more of the meat filling over the top. Makes about 8 servings.

## Chirrasquillas

This interesting main dish, made with tortillas and ground beef, is from Costa Rica. Costa Ricans garnish the dish with fried plantains. You might try green bananas, if you like the idea; slice them and fry them in the same fat. Also serve a Spanish-style hot tomato sauce, refried beans, and fried chorizo sausages.

1 large onion, chopped
2 tablespoons lard or shortening
1 pound ground beef
1 teaspoon salt
Dash of pepper
Pinch of oregano
1 small clove garlic, puréed (optional)
12 tortillas
1 cup beer or water
1 cup flour
½ teaspoon salt
3 eggs
Fat for frying

Sauté onion in lard or shortening until wilted. Add beef, the 1 teaspoon salt, pepper, oregano, and garlic. Cook until the meat browns, mashing with a fork to dispel lumps. Cool and divide the mixture among the 12 tortillas, putting spoonfuls on the center of each. Fold over as you would turnovers and fasten with toothpicks.

Make a batter by beating together the beer or water, flour, ½ teaspoon salt, and eggs. Dip the folded tortillas into this batter, one at a time, and fry in deep fat at 365° to 370° or in 1½ inches of salad oil in a large frying pan. Makes 12 chirrasquillas.

# *West Indian Dinner

Mushroom Soup
Jamaican Meat-stuffed Pumpkin (*see recipe opposite*)
Tossed Greens Salad
Hot Buttered French Bread
West Indies Parfait with Strawberries

In Jamaica, meat-stuffed pumpkin is usually offered as one of many dishes on a long and well-laden buffet table. It makes an ideal main dish for an autumn buffet supper or informal Halloween dinner. The creamy parfait dessert is one you make early in the day and chill.

### Mushroom Soup

Try one of the dehydrated mushroom soups to start this meal. Add 1 teaspoon sherry to each cup of soup and sprinkle each serving with minced parsley.

### West Indies Parfait with Strawberries

1½ cups light cream
¼ cup butter or margarine
3 eggs, separated
½ cup dark brown sugar, firmly packed

1 envelope (1 tablespoon) unflavored gelatin
¼ cup water
Salt
¾ teaspoon rum flavoring (or rum to taste)
¼ cup granulated sugar
Sliced sugared fresh strawberries, or drained frozen strawberries

In the top of a double boiler, heat to scalding light cream and butter. Beat egg yolks with the brown sugar, blend in some of the hot mixture, then return all to double boiler. Cook over simmering water, stirring, until thickened. Soften gelatin in water; blend with hot mixture until dissolved. Flavor with a dash of salt and the rum flavoring. Chill until softly set. Whip egg whites until stiff; gradually beat in granulated sugar until peaks are stiff and glossy. Fold into chilled mixture. Spoon into parfait glasses, making alternating layers of sliced sugared strawberries and parfait mixture; or reserve the berries to spoon on top later. Chill. Makes 6 to 8 servings.

# Stuffed Green Pepper Rings

Olives and corn are the surprise ingredients in this interesting variation of stuffed peppers.

4 large green peppers
2 pounds ground beef
1 can (12 oz.) whole kernel corn, or
   1 package frozen corn, thawed
1 large can (1 lb., 13 oz.) tomatoes
2 cans (4½ oz. each) chopped ripe olives
2 teaspoons salt
½ teaspoon pepper
12 whole pitted ripe olives
4 ounces (4 slices) mild processed cheese

Wash, cut out stem ends, and seed green peppers. Slice into 3 wide rings to make 12 in all. Arrange in a greased shallow baking dish. In a frying pan over medium heat, cook the meat, stirring, until lightly browned. Add corn, tomatoes, chopped olives, salt, and pepper.

Fill green pepper rings with the meat mixture; press a whole olive in the center of each. Top each with a piece of cheese. Cover baking dish with lid or foil. Bake in a moderate oven (350°) for 45 minutes. Uncover and continue baking for 15 minutes. Makes 6 generous servings.

## Beef and Rice in Grape Leaves

Stuffed grape leaves, which are called *dolmathes* in Greek, can be prepared with a variety of fillings. In this recipe, the filling is ground beef. You can find canned grape leaves in specialty food shops; or you can use cabbage leaves in place of the grape leaves (let them stand in boiling water until they are quite pliable, then remove from water and trim away the thick stem).

1 pound lean ground beef
1 large onion, chopped
½ cup uncooked rice
3 tablespoons butter or margarine
½ cup chopped parsley
¼ cup chopped mint
2 teaspoons salt
1 teaspoon pepper
1 teaspoon dill weed
3 or 4 dozen grape leaves, canned or fresh
1 cup water
3 eggs
3 tablespoons lemon juice

Combine ground beef, onion, rice, butter, parsley, mint, salt, pepper, and dill. Wash grape leaves in hot water; drain on paper toweling. Spread each leaf on a flat surface with the under side up and the stem end toward you; cut off stem. Place about 2 teaspoons of filling near the stem end, then fold the sides of the leaf over the filling and roll away from you. Continue until all the filling is used. Place the rolls in a large kettle (at least 6-quart size) on a layer of grape leaves. Add water and place a heat-proof plate on top of the rolls to prevent them from breaking apart. Cover pan and simmer for 40 minutes, or until rice is tender. Drain rolls, saving the cooking liquid. Beat eggs until fluffy and add lemon juice, 1 tablespoon at a time. Gradually stir in the cooking liquid from the dolmathes. Pour sauce over the rolls. Makes 8 to 10 servings (about 40 rolls).

*Grape leaves are rolled around a filling of beef and rice to make this delicious version of Greek dolmathes.*

## Biscuit Pinwheels

Each serving of this dinner roll is a biscuit pinwheel filled with potatoes, vegetables, and meat.

2 cups biscuit mix
⅔ cup milk
1 cup well-seasoned mashed potatoes
1 pound ground beef
1 tablespoon salad oil
1 cup ground raw carrots
½ cup ground onion
1 teaspoon salt
¼ teaspoon pepper
3 cups hot cheese, tomato, or mushroom sauce

Combine biscuit mix and milk to make a soft dough. Roll out into an 8 by 12-inch rectangle on a lightly floured board. Spread the potatoes evenly over one-third of the biscuit dough, and roll that third toward the center. Brown meat in oil until crumbly; mix in carrots, onion, salt, and pepper; spread over the remaining dough. Roll up and place in a greased baking pan. Bake in a moderately hot oven (375°) for 45 minutes, or until roll is golden brown. Slice and serve with a hot cheese, tomato, or mushroom sauce. Makes 6 servings.

## Chili Beef Stack  *(see suggested menu below)* ✳

½ medium-sized onion, chopped
½ medium-sized green pepper, chopped
1½ pounds ground beef
1 small can (3 or 4 oz.) sliced mushrooms, drained
2 tablespoons shortening
2 cans (8 oz. each) tomato sauce
½ teaspoon chili powder
½ teaspoon dry mustard
1 teaspoon salt
½ teaspoon pepper
¼ teaspoon garlic salt

*Pancakes:*
1 egg
1½ cups milk
¾ cup cornmeal
¾ cup whole wheat flour
½ teaspoon salt
1 tablespoon baking powder
1 tablespoon salad oil
Grated Parmesan cheese

Sauté onion, green pepper, ground beef, and mushrooms in melted shortening, stirring occasionally with a fork until meat is browned. Stir in tomato sauce, chili powder, mustard, salt, pepper, and garlic salt, and simmer over low heat for 15 minutes.

Meanwhile, make pancakes as follows: Beat egg lightly and beat in milk. Gradually stir in cornmeal, whole wheat flour, salt, and baking powder, and beat until batter is smooth. Blend in oil. Cook pancakes on both sides on a hot, greased griddle until golden brown. Makes 18 pancakes 4 to 5 inches in diameter.

For each serving, spoon meat sauce between and on top of a stack of three pancakes. Sprinkle with grated Parmesan cheese. Makes 6 servings.

---

## ✳ *South of the Border Lunch*

Chili Beef Stack *(see recipe above)*
Green Salad with Slices of Avocado and Green Onions
French Dressing
Ginger-Lemon Ice

This luncheon has a Mexican theme, with cornmeal pancakes stacked like a double-decker sandwich with a filling of pleasantly hot, chili-seasoned meat sauce. The Ginger-Lemon Ice dessert is a cooling contrast.

### *Ginger-Lemon Ice*

For each serving, surround 1 scoop of lemon sherbet with 5 or 6 canned mandarin orange sections. Sprinkle with about 1 teaspoon minced crystallized ginger and a few gratings of orange peel. Pass a small pitcher of freshly squeezed orange juice to pour over the sherbet.

## Banana Meat Rolls

Individual meat rolls, centered with a whole banana, are company fare.

½ cup chopped onion
1 teaspoon minced garlic
1 tablespoon shortening
1 pound ground beef
2 slices soft bread, cut in cubes
2 eggs, beaten
½ cup milk
2 medium-sized cooked potatoes, finely chopped
2 teaspoons salt
½ teaspoon pepper
1 teaspoon prepared horseradish
Dash each of sage, thyme, marjoram,
    savory, and celery salt
2 teaspoons minced parsley
4 bananas
Lemon juice

Sauté onion and garlic in shortening, and add to ground beef. Combine bread cubes with eggs, milk, potatoes, and seasonings. Add meat mixture and blend thoroughly. (Mixture is quite soft but easy to handle.) Sprinkle bananas with lemon juice and pat ¼ of the meat mixture evenly and firmly around each banana. Arrange the 4 loaves in a flat baking dish. Bake in a moderate oven (350°) for 30 minutes. Makes 4 servings.

## Samosas

In this Pakistani recipe, a blend of curry spices seasons the filling for deep-fried pastry.

1 pound lean ground beef
1 small onion, finely chopped
2 tablespoons butter or margarine
1 teaspoon finely chopped green chili pepper
½ teaspoon mashed or minced fresh ginger root
    or ⅛ teaspoon powdered ginger
½ teaspoon salt
⅛ teaspoon each cardamon, coriander,
    turmeric, and paprika
Pinch each of caraway and cumin seeds
4 whole cloves
½ cinnamon stick
2 whole black peppers
½ cup water
1 cup flour
½ cup whole wheat flour
½ teaspoon salt
2 tablespoons butter or margarine
4 tablespoons (¼ cup) water

Sauté ground beef and onion in butter until onion is tender. Season with chili pepper, ginger root, and salt. With a mortar and pestle, grind together cardamon, coriander, turmeric, paprika, caraway and cumin seeds, cloves, cinnamon stick, and black peppers. Make a paste of ground spices and water, then pour over meat. Cover and cook for 20 minutes, or until most of the water has evaporated.

While meat is cooking, sift flour, measure, then sift again with whole wheat flour and salt. Blend in butter until mixture is crumbly. With a fork, lightly stir in just enough water so the mixture holds together. Divide dough into 18 portions; on a lightly floured board, roll out each portion into a disk ⅛ inch thick and approximately 3 inches in diameter. As you roll out each round, spoon about 1 tablespoon of the cooked meat filling onto one half of the pastry round; fold over the other half, moisten edge with water, and crimp with a fork. Cook in hot deep fat for 3 to 4 minutes, or until golden brown. Drain on absorbent paper. Serve immediately. Makes 18 samosas.

## Empanadas de Carne

South American *empanadas* are an excellent choice for a casual buffet dinner or party. You can prepare them in advance, freeze them, and then cook them shortly before serving, and you can keep them warm in the oven for an hour or even reheat them without affecting their quality.

4 cups unsifted flour
2 teaspoons salt
1⅓ cups shortening
⅔ cup cold water
1½ pounds ground round
1 clove garlic, mashed
1 teaspoon salt
¼ teaspoon pepper
⅓ cup chopped onion
2 tablespoons butter
2 medium-sized tomatoes, halved and thinly sliced
½ cup raisins
1 can (2¼ oz.) sliced olives

Measure flour into a large mixing bowl; mix in salt. Cut in shortening with a pastry blender or 2 knives until mixture is the consistency of cornmeal. Sprinkle water over top and mix in with a fork. Shape dough into 3 balls; chill for 30 minutes or longer.

Season meat with the garlic, salt, and pepper. Sauté onion in butter until golden; stir in meat, and cook until brown. Remove from heat; stir in tomatoes, raisins, and olives. Roll out each ball of dough into a very thin sheet (about 1/16 inch). Use a small plate (6 to 7 inches in diameter) as a pattern to cut out rounds of dough. Spoon 2 to 3 tablespoons of meat filling on one side of each round; brush water around the edge with your finger. Fold free half over filling; pinch edges together and crimp. Slip empanadas into 2 inches of hot cooking oil (400°) in a frying pan. Cook for 2½ to 3 minutes per side, or until golden. Use tongs to turn and remove empanadas to a cooky sheet lined with a triple thickness of paper toweling. Keep in a warm oven (175°) until time to serve. Makes 24 empanadas.

To freeze uncooked empanadas, stack tightly in a box or pan and cover with foil. When ready to deep-fry, spread them on a cooky sheet and thaw at room temperature for about 2 hours, then cook as directed above. To reheat cooked empanadas

*You can prepare empanadas ahead of time for a party meal. Serve them with a green salad and white wine.*

that have been stored in the refrigerator, place them on a cooky sheet and heat in a moderately slow oven (300°) for 12 minutes.

## Beef Tomato Swirls

A "jelly roll" technique wraps the sauce into every swirled serving of this entrée.

2 pounds lean ground beef
2 eggs, slightly beaten
1 can (10½ oz.) tomato soup
2 teaspoons salt
¼ teaspoon pepper
½ cup finely chopped onion
½ cup chopped green pepper
1 tablespoon Worcestershire
2 cups fresh bread crumbs
1½ cups shredded Cheddar cheese

Combine the meat with eggs, half the can of tomato soup, 1 teaspoon of the salt, and ⅛ teaspoon of the pepper. Pat the mixture out on a piece of waxed paper into an oblong about 15 by 8 inches. Combine the remaining soup, salt, and pepper with onion, green pepper, Worcestershire, bread crumbs, and cheese; spread over the meat. Roll up like a jelly roll, using the waxed paper to lift the meat. Cut into 1½-inch-thick slices. Arrange in a greased shallow baking pan. Bake in a moderately slow oven (325°) for 45 minutes. Makes 10 slices.

## Greek Pastry and Meat Pie

This is a hearty main dish made with a filling of ground beef, fresh parsley, and onion, layered between sheets of fila dough. Cut it in large diamond shapes and serve it warm as a main dish, or cut it into tiny diamonds to serve as hors d'oeuvres.

1½ pounds lean ground beef
6 tablespoons butter
3 large onions, finely chopped
1½ cups chopped fresh parsley
2 eggs, beaten
1½ teaspoons salt
1½ teaspoons pepper
1 cup (½ pound) butter, melted
1 pound fila (available in 1-pound packages
 at Greek food stores)

Lightly brown ground beef in about 2 tablespoons of the butter. Sauté onions in the remaining 4 tablespoons butter just until golden and limp. Mix together cooked beef, onions, parsley, eggs, salt, and pepper. Separate sheets of fila dough into two equal portions of 6 to 8 sheets each. Brush bottom of a 10 by 15-inch baking pan with part of the 1 cup of melted butter.

Allowing excess dough to hang over edges of the pan, arrange layers of half the sheets of dough in the bottom of pan; brush each sheet with butter. Trim off excess fila around pan edges. Spread meat mixture evenly over dough; top with remaining sheets of fila, brushing each with melted butter. Trim off fila to within ½-inch of pan edges; tuck top layers down inside pan. Cut top layers of unbaked pastry diagonally across pan to make diamond shapes about 2 inches wide, 3 inches long (do not cut through bottom layers of pastry). Bake in a slow oven (300°) for 1 hour, 20 minutes. Serve warm. Makes about 12 servings.

*Flaky Greek pastry with a filling of ground beef makes an attractive main dish to serve to guests.*

## Beef and Oysters on a Plank

*(see suggested menu opposite)* ✳

1½ pounds ground chuck
½ cup soft bread crumbs
2 tablespoons chopped parsley
1 egg, slightly beaten
¼ cup milk
1 teaspoon salt
1 teaspoon sugar
⅛ teaspoon pepper
1 medium-sized onion, finely chopped
1 green pepper, cut in thin rings
1 cup catsup (with extra seasonings)
1 container (about 12 oz.) oysters
3 cups hot mashed potatoes
1 cup cooked carrots
1 cup cooked peas
¼ cup melted butter

Combine beef with bread crumbs, parsley, egg, milk, salt, sugar, and pepper; shape into one large patty about 1 inch thick, and center on a buttered heat-proof platter. Layer the onion and green pepper on top of the meat. Pour catsup over meat. Bake in a hot oven (400°) for 10 minutes (longer if you like meat well done). Arrange oysters over meat; surround with generous mounds of the potatoes, making hollows with a spoon. Fill hollows with combined carrots and peas. Sprinkle all with melted butter. Set in a very hot oven (475°) for 10 to 15 minutes. Serve with lemon wedges and chopped parsley, if you wish. Makes 4 to 6 servings.

# *A Planked Dinner for Guests

Fruit Frappé
Beef and Oysters on a Plank (*see recipe opposite*)
Mashed Potatoes    Carrots with Peas
Hot Crescent Rolls
Chocolate Dainty

Here's an idea for a dramatic yet very easy-to-prepare guest dinner. The Fruit Frappé and dessert can be completed early in the day. Make the rolls from your favorite recipe or buy the refrigerated kind.

## Fruit Frappé

1 large banana, finely diced
Grated peel and juice of 1 lemon
Grated peel and juice of 1 orange
½ cup drained, canned crushed pineapple
¼ cup sugar
2 cups ginger ale

Blend together in a bowl diced banana, lemon and orange peel and juice, pineapple, sugar, and ginger ale. Pour into a freezer tray and freeze for 1½ to 2 hours or until icy, stirring frequently. Store in freezer, covered, until serving time. Serve in small, chilled bowls as a first course. Makes 4 to 6 servings.

## Chocolate Dainty

⅓ cup butter
¾ cup sifted powdered sugar
3 eggs, separated
2 squares (1 oz. each) unsweetened chocolate, melted
½ teaspoon vanilla
¼ cup very fine, dry bread crumbs
Whipped cream
Vanilla
Nutmeg

Cream together butter and sugar until fluffy. Beat egg yolks and combine with melted chocolate, vanilla, and bread crumbs. Blend into butter and sugar mixture. Beat egg whites until stiff and fold in. Evenly divide ⅔ of chocolate mixture between two buttered 8-inch cake pans; smooth surface. Bake in a moderately slow oven (325°) for 20 minutes, or until set. Remove from pans and chill. Spread remaining ⅓ of unbaked chocolate mixture between layers. Decorate with puffs of whipped cream, sweetened and flavored with vanilla. Sprinkle with nutmeg. Chill until ready to serve. Cut in wedges. Makes 6 to 8 servings.

## Meat-Vegetable Pasties

These are good for luncheon or supper, or as a lunch box treat. You can make them ahead and freeze them; remove from freezer and allow to thaw at room temperature, then reheat them in a 300° oven for about 15 minutes. Serve them plain, or with a mushroom gravy or cheese sauce.

2 medium-sized onions, chopped
4 tablespoons butter or margarine
2 pounds ground round
3 teaspoons salt
½ teaspoon pepper
½ teaspoon allspice
1 small head cabbage, chopped
1 package (14 oz.) hot roll mix
1 egg
2 tablespoons milk

Brown onions in butter and add meat; cook, stirring, until redness disappears from beef. Add salt, pepper, allspice, and cabbage and simmer for 45 minutes, covered, stirring occassionally. Set aside to cool.

Prepare roll mix according to directions on the package. When dough has risen sufficiently, **turn** onto a floured board and roll out to about ¼-inch thickness, making a rectangle 16 by 24 inches. Cut dough with a sharp knife into six 8-inch squares. Pack cooled filling into a ½-cup measure and invert on center of each dough square. Bring corners together at center of the top of the square and pinch edges to seal, making 4 diagonal seams. Place on a well-greased cooky sheet. Combine egg with milk, mixing with a fork until blended. Brush pasties with egg-milk mixture and bake in a moderate oven (350°) for 30 minutes or until golden brown. Serve hot or cooled. Makes 6 pasties.

## Sicilian Meat Roll

This delightful dish called *Farso Margo* comes from Sicily. Lean beefsteak, stuffed with ground beef and savories, is rolled and cooked until tender, then cooled and served in slices with a salad and crusty bread. You can also make it with veal steak, adding a few anchovy fillets and green olives to the stuffing.

2 to 2½-pound piece round steak,
    about 1-inch thick
1 pound ground beef
1 clove garlic, minced
¼ cup minced parsley
¼ cup grated Parmesan cheese
½ medium-sized onion, chopped
¼ cup soft bread crumbs
2 eggs, beaten
1½ teaspoons salt
Freshly ground black pepper
2 tablespoons milk or wine
¼ cup olive oil or salad oil
½ cup red wine
½ cup tomato juice
½ cup water or stock
1 carrot, sliced
1 onion, sliced
Herb bouquet (bay leaf, parsley,
    marjoram, and rosemary)

Pound round steak until it is ½-inch thick; trim fat. Spread with this mixture: Combine ground beef with garlic, parsley, Parmesan cheese, chopped onion, bread crumbs, eggs, salt, pepper, and milk or wine. (If you wish, sprinkle on chopped hard-cooked egg or chopped ham or tongue.)

Roll up the meat like a jelly roll; tie securely at the ends and loosely in two or three places (it will look like a large sausage). Brown meat in olive oil on all sides, using a pan not much larger than the meat roll. Add wine, tomato juice, water, sliced carrot, sliced onion, and herb bouquet. Cover tightly and simmer for 1¼ hours, or until fork-tender, adding water if necessary. Chill. Slice the chilled meat roll and serve with or without the sauce (skim fat from sauce before serving). Makes 6 to 8 servings.

## Finnish Meat Rolls

The meat mixture is similar to the one used for tiny Finnish meat balls, but shaping the rolls takes much less time. You can make and fill the rolls, ready for baking, then store them in your freezer. Thaw completely before cooking.

1 pound ground chuck
½ cup mashed potatoes
2 tablespoons fine dry bread crumbs
1 egg
1 teaspoon salt
¼ teaspoon ground allspice
⅓ cup minced onion
⅓ cup minced pickled beets
⅓ cup finely chopped parsley
¼ teaspoon salt
Dash of pepper
8 slices bacon

Combine thoroughly the ground chuck, mashed potatoes, bread crumbs, egg, the 1 teaspoon salt, and allspice, making a smooth mixture about the same consistency as for meat balls. Moisten a piece of waxed paper about 18 inches long, and spread the meat mixture onto it to make a rectangle 8 by 12 inches. (The paper will not slip if you moisten the surface beneath it, too.) Cut the meat rectangle into 8 even parts.

Combine onion, beets, parsley, the ¼ teaspoon salt, and pepper; spoon some of this filling onto the center of each meat portion, and roll up. Wrap a bacon slice around each meat roll. Arrange rolls in a casserole, slightly separated so the bacon will cook crisp. (You can refrigerate or freeze the rolls at this stage.) Bake in a moderately hot oven (375°) for 30 to 35 minutes, or until bacon is browned and crisp on top. Makes 4 servings.

## Rolled Meat Pancakes

This is a make-ahead recipe that is especially good for serving large groups. You wrap thin pancakes around a meat and spinach filling, then top each serving with tomato sauce and cheese before baking. You can fill the pancakes in advance and store them, covered, in the refrigerator; spoon the tomato sauce and cheese over the pancakes just before you bake them.

Rolled meat pancakes (below) can be made ahead, then topped with sauce and cheese just before you bake them.

2 pounds ground beef
1 pound bulk sausage
2 medium-sized onions, finely chopped
3 cloves garlic, minced or mashed
4 packages (10 oz. each) frozen chopped spinach, cooked and well drained
Salt to taste
6 eggs
¾ teaspoon salt
3 cups milk
2 cups flour
Butter or margarine
6 cans (8 oz. each) tomato sauce
2 cups shredded sharp Cheddar cheese

Brown meats with onion and garlic until crumbly. Mix in spinach; salt to taste. Beat eggs with salt and milk. Sift flour, measure, and sift into the egg mixture; beat until well blended. Pour about 2 tablespoons batter into buttered, hot 5 to 7-inch frying pan; tilt pan so batter covers bottom. When brown on one side, remove. Continue until batter is used, buttering pan as needed.

Divide filling between pancakes, and roll each. Place in three 9 by 13-inch baking pans. Pour tomato sauce over rolls; sprinkle with cheese. Bake in a moderate oven (350°) for 30 minutes (40 to 45 minutes, if refrigerated). Makes 18 to 27 servings, with 2 or 3 rolls per serving.

*Hearty soup, filled with chopped vegetables and browned meat balls, is a delicious and satisfying lunch or supper for the family. Recipe and suggested menu, page 75.*

# HEARTY SOUPS

## *these are meals in themselves*

## Meat Ball and Vegetable Soup

This richly flavored soup is almost a stew, it's so full of tender meat balls and vegetables. It tastes even better reheated; so if your family is small, you can still prepare the full recipe and freeze the extra soup for future meals.

1 large beef knucklebone
2 or 3 marrow bones
½ cup pearl barley
2 quarts water
1 can (1 lb., 13 oz.) tomatoes, cut in pieces
1 pound ground beef chuck
½ cup cracker meal
1 egg
2 teaspoons salt
½ teaspoon pepper
4 medium-sized carrots, cut in pieces
3 stalks celery with tops, sliced crosswise
1 medium-sized onion, chopped
2 cloves garlic, minced or mashed
2 small zucchini, thinly sliced
½ cup fresh or frozen peas

Pressure-cook bones and barley in water for 1 hour. Remove from heat and let cool to reduce pressure. Discard bones. (Or cover and simmer for 3 hours.) Add water to make 2 quarts total. Add tomatoes and simmer slowly as you prepare meat balls. Mix together meat, cracker meal, egg, 1 teaspoon of the salt, and ¼ teaspoon of the pepper. Shape into tiny meat balls about 1 inch in diameter and drop into simmering broth. Add carrots, celery, onion, garlic, and remaining 1 teaspoon salt and ¼ teaspoon pepper. Cook slowly for 45 minutes. Add the sliced zucchini and peas, and continue cooking for an additional 15 minutes. Makes about 8 to 10 servings.

## Cauliflower Soup

Unlike most other meat ball soups, this creamy cauliflower version is made with milk. It originated in the Netherlands.

1 medium-sized head cauliflower
Milk
½ cup flour
¼ cup (4 tablespoons) butter or margarine
1 pound beef, ground twice
1 medium-sized onion, finely chopped
2 tablespoons minced parsley
1 egg, slightly beaten
1 teaspoon salt
¼ teaspoon pepper
⅛ teaspoon nutmeg
Salt and pepper
Chopped chives or parsley

Trim tiny flowerets from cauliflower and set aside. Cut remaining cauliflower into pieces and cook until tender in boiling salted water. Drain and put through a sieve. Measure and add enough milk to make 2 quarts. Blend some of this mixture with flour to make a smooth paste, and stir back into cauliflower and milk. Add butter.

Heat over hot water until thickened, stirring occasionally. Meanwhile, mix ground beef with onion, parsley, egg, 1 teaspoon salt, and ¼ teaspoon pepper; shape into meat balls about ¾ to 1 inch in diameter. Drop meat balls and cauliflowerets into the hot soup, a few at a time, and cook for 20 minutes, or until meat balls are cooked. Season with nutmeg and salt and pepper to taste. Sprinkle each serving with snipped chives or finely chopped parsley. Makes 6 to 8 servings.

## Beef and Carrot Soup

You don't need a soup bone to make this soup laced with carrot and onion because ground beef supplies the meat flavor.

1 pound ground beef
1½ cups coarsely grated onion
   (about 3 medium-sized onions)
6 cups water
1½ cups coarsely grated carrot
   (about 4 medium-sized carrots)
1½ teaspoons salt
½ teaspoon pepper
4 tablespoons (¼ cup) butter or margarine
⅓ cup flour
1½ cups milk
½ teaspoon salt
¼ teaspoon pepper
Grated Parmesan cheese

Brown beef and onion together for 5 minutes, stirring with a fork to crumble meat. While meat is browning, heat water to boiling, then add meat, onion, pan drippings, carrot, the 1½ teaspoons salt, and the ½ teaspoon pepper. Cover and simmer for 1 hour. Melt butter in a saucepan; blend in flour until smooth; add milk, and cook, stirring constantly, until smooth and thick. Season with the ½ teaspoon salt and the ¼ teaspoon pepper. Just before serving stir the cream sauce into the ground beef mixture and heat until piping hot. Sprinkle 1 tablespoon grated cheese over each serving.

## Armenian Meat Ball Soup

This is an adaptation of a recipe called Royal or Victory Soup in which the meat balls are made with venison instead of beef.

½ pound ground round or chuck
½ cup quick-cooking cracked wheat (uncooked)
¼ cup finely chopped onion
¼ cup finely chopped parsley
5 cans (14 oz. each) chicken broth, or
   1½ large cans (46 oz. size) chicken broth
⅓ cup lemon juice
3 eggs
Salt and pepper to taste

Combine ground beef with cracked wheat, onion, and parsley; form into tiny balls about the size of filbert nuts. Heat the chicken broth to boiling, and drop in meat balls; simmer, covered, for about 1 hour. Just before you are ready to serve, combine lemon juice with eggs in a large heat-proof bowl; beat until thoroughly blended. Using a slotted spoon, remove meat balls from broth and distribute among individual soup bowls. Slowly pour hot broth into egg mixture, beating constantly. Taste, and add salt and pepper if needed. Ladle into bowls and serve immediately. Makes 10 to 12 servings.

## Hamburger Soup

This very meaty soup is certainly a main dish. Make it in a large kettle and serve with a hot, crusty bread for a family lunch or supper.

2 pounds ground beef
2 tablespoons olive oil or salad oil
½ teaspoon salt
¼ teaspoon pepper
¼ teaspoon oregano
¼ teaspoon basil
⅛ teaspoon seasoned salt
1 package onion soup mix (for 3 or 4 servings)
6 cups boiling water
1 can (8 oz.) tomato sauce
1 tablespoon soy sauce
1 cup celery, sliced crosswise
¼ cup celery leaves, torn in large pieces
1 cup sliced carrots
⅓ cup dried split peas
1 cup elbow macaroni
Parmesan cheese

In a large saucepan or kettle with a tight fitting lid, brown meat in oil. Add salt, pepper, oregano, basil, seasoned salt, and onion soup mix. Stir in boiling water, tomato sauce, and soy sauce. Cover and simmer for about 15 minutes. Meanwhile, prepare celery, celery leaves, and carrots; then add to simmering mixture with the split peas and continue to cook for 30 minutes. Add macaroni and simmer for 30 minutes longer, adding more water if necessary. Pass grated Parmesan cheese to be sprinkled over individual servings. Makes 6 to 8 servings.

## Hearty Meat Ball Soup   *(see suggested menu below)*

During the last 20 minutes of cooking, put browned meat balls into this vegetable soup. It makes a delicious and satisfying lunch or supper.

2 quarts water
2 fresh tomatoes, peeled and cut in small pieces
1 cup chopped carrots
1 cup chopped celery
1 large onion, chopped
2 tablespoons chopped parsley
¼ teaspoon Worcestershire
Liquid hot-pepper seasoning
3 teaspoons salt
¼ teaspoon oregano
1 pound lean ground beef
1 slice boiled ham, chopped
1 slice bacon, cooked and chopped
½ cup fine cracker crumbs
2 tablespoons Parmesan cheese
1 teaspoon chopped parsley
1 egg, slightly beaten
2 teaspoons basil
2 tablespoons salad oil

In a pan mix the water, tomatoes, carrots, celery, onion, parsley, Worcestershire, a few drops of liquid hot-pepper seasoning, 2 teaspoons of the salt, and oregano. Cover and simmer for 1 hour. Mix together the ground beef, ham, bacon, cracker crumbs, cheese, parsley, remaining 1 teaspoon salt, egg, and basil until lightly blended. Shape into meat balls, about 1 inch in diameter. Brown on all sides in the hot oil. Drop meat balls into soup; cook for 20 minutes. Makes 6 to 8 servings.

## *Meat Ball Soup Lunch

Hearty Meat Ball Soup *(see recipe above)*
Green Salad
Cornbread
Hot Caramel Peaches

Serve this to your family for lunch or late supper. Hot cornbread (from a mix or your own recipe) and green salad complement the hearty soup. A quick peach dessert finishes the meal. Heat the peach halves over low heat while your family enjoys the rest of the meal; then assemble the dessert and serve immediately.

### Hot Caramel Peaches
1 can (about 1 lb., 14 oz.) cling peach halves
¼ cup brown sugar
¾ cup sour cream
Cinnamon

In a saucepan, heat peaches in their own syrup. Place each hot peach half in a small dessert dish and top with 2 teaspoons brown sugar and 2 tablespoons sour cream. Sprinkle with cinnamon. Makes 6 servings.

*Walnut halves garnish this beef appetizer (see page 78) and toasted chopped walnuts contribute flavor to the meat. Serve with an assortment of breads and crisp crackers.*

# SAVORY APPETIZERS

## *they're made from ground beef*

## Beef Tartare Loaf

Simple as raw beef appetizers are to prepare and serve, the key to their excellence is the use of the highest quality beef. To serve, heap on toasted whole wheat, pumpernickel, rye bread, or crackers.

5 pounds sirloin or other tender beef,
    trimmed and finely ground
4 or 5 egg yolks, slightly beaten
3 medium-sized onions, finely minced
5 teaspoons salt
1 teaspoon freshly ground pepper
½ cup minced parsley
Chives
Capers

Mix beef with egg yolks, onions, salt, pepper, and parsley. When thoroughly blended, form into a loaf or long roll, and sprinkle with minced chives. Stud with whole capers. Makes about 50 appetizers.

## Jack's Caps

Here's a hot hors d'oeuvre that will please anyone who likes mushrooms. Serve these as a first course at the table, or use smaller mushrooms and serve as finger food with plenty of napkins.

16 large mushrooms (about 2 inches in diameter)
½ cup soy sauce
½ pound lean ground beef
¼ cup minced green peppers
2 tablespoons fine dry bread crumbs
1 egg yolk
1 tablespoon minced onion
½ clove garlic, crushed
¼ teaspoon salt
¼ teaspoon pepper

Remove stems from mushrooms and scoop out a little of the flesh to form a depression inside each mushroom cap. Save stems and pieces; marinate caps in soy for about 1 hour. If soy does not cover them, turn them occasionally. Finely chop mushroom stems and pieces and mix with all remaining ingredients. Remove mushroom caps from soy, drain, and fill with meat mixture, mounding up the surface. Brush meat with soy. Broil in the oven until meat and mushrooms are done to your liking (8 to 10 minutes), basting frequently with the soy. If you have to hold them for any length of time, they can be reheated in a moderate oven (350°). Serve at least 2 mushrooms per person.

## Beef and Walnut Ball

Simplicity of flavors—fresh beef and lightly toasted walnuts—distinguish this appetizer.

½ cup chopped walnuts
1 tablespoon melted butter
1 pound ground round
About 2 tablespoons sherry
Salt and pepper to taste
Walnut halves

Stir chopped walnuts in the melted butter, then brown lightly in a moderate oven (350°); drain on paper towels, and add to ground round. Stir in enough sherry to moisten; add salt and pepper. Mold into a large round on serving platter. Press walnut halves into top of ball to garnish. Makes 12 to 16 appetizers.

## Beef and Mushroom Appetizer

Here's another delicious "cannibal canapé" made from uncooked beef.

¼ pound fresh mushrooms
1 pound ground round
Tops of 6 green onions, sliced
Salt and pepper to taste

Chop mushrooms into chunks and add to raw beef. Mash together lightly with a fork. Add onion, salt, and pepper. Pile on crisp bread. Makes 12 to 16 appetizers.

## Spicy Meat Balls

Curry is the special flavor touch in these delicious appetizer meat balls.

1 onion, finely chopped
1 cup fine dry bread crumbs
2 pounds ground round or sirloin
3 eggs
½ teaspoon salt
¼ teaspoon pepper
½ teaspoon seasoning salt
¾ teaspoon curry powder, or to taste
¼ cup grated Parmesan cheese
½ teaspoon Worcestershire
2 cloves garlic
1 cup flour
Salad oil or shortening
1 cup red table wine
½ cup beef consommé
2 small cans (8 oz. each) tomato sauce
⅛ to ¼ teaspoon oregano (optional)

Add onion and bread crumbs to meat, mix thoroughly, then add the eggs and mix again. Add salt, pepper, seasoning salt, curry powder, Parmesan cheese, and Worcestershire, and again mix well by hand until blended in. Crush 1 clove of garlic and mix in. Roll meat into small balls about 1½ inches in diameter; roll lightly in flour. Crush the remaining clove of garlic, and add to oil in a large frying pan. Fill pan with as many meat balls as it will take; cook, turning with a fork, for about 8 minutes, or until well browned on all sides.

Meanwhile, combine wine, consommé, tomato sauce, and oregano in a large saucepan and simmer while the first meat balls are frying. As meat balls are done, add them to the sauce and continue to simmer all for about 25 to 35 minutes. Add meat balls and sauce to chafing dish, and serve with toothpicks for spearing. If sauce needs more liquid, add more of the consommé. Makes about 80 small meat balls.

## Smoky Meat Balls

These small browned meat balls simmer in a smoky-flavored tomato sauce. Serve them in a chafing dish with a supply of fancy picks handy so your guests can spear them. You can make the meat balls ahead and freeze them, if you wish; when ready to use, simmer them in the sauce for about 20 minutes, or until they are heated through.

2 pounds lean ground beef
¼ cup chopped onion
1 teaspoon salt
¼ teaspoon pepper
¼ teaspoon garlic salt
½ cup fine cracker crumbs
1 egg
¼ cup milk
2 tablespoons salad oil
1 bottle (1 lb., 2 oz.) smoky-type barbecue sauce
1 cup water

Mix together until lightly blended the ground beef, onion, salt, pepper, garlic salt, cracker crumbs, egg, and milk. Shape into meat balls about the size of walnuts. Brown on all sides in hot salad oil. In a large pan, mix together until blended the barbecue sauce and water. Place the browned meat balls in this sauce and simmer for 15 minutes. Pour meat balls and sauce into a chafing dish, and serve with small picks. Makes about 8 dozen small meat balls.

## Gingered Meat Balls

This recipe makes about 175 small bite-sized meat balls. Mix and shape the balls well ahead of party time. If you don't have a chafing dish or heated tray in which to serve them, turn your oven to its

*Piping hot meat balls, served from a chafing dish, are a favorite addition to any party snack table.*

lowest setting and keep part of the meat balls warm while serving the others.

¾ cup soy sauce
¾ cup water
2 small cloves garlic, mashed
2 teaspoons ground ginger
3 pounds ground chuck or round steak
Parsley for garnish

In a large bowl, combine the soy sauce, water, garlic, and ginger; mix until blended. Add the ground meat and blend lightly but thoroughly. Lift out spoonfuls of the meat mixture and lightly form with your hands into balls under 1 inch in diameter. If you plan to cook the meat balls later, cover with clear plastic film and refrigerate. To cook the meat balls, arrange in a single layer in a large baking pan. Put into a slow oven (275°) and bake uncovered for about 15 minutes; turn once during the baking time. Serve hot with toothpicks to spear each one. Garnish the serving tray with parsley sprays. Makes about 175 appetizers.

# INDEX

**Photographers:** Clyde Childress, page 2; Robert Cox, pages 33, 36; Blair Stapp, page 30; Darrow M. Watt, pages 8, 11, 16, 38, 40, 47, 52, 58, 60, 64, 67, 68, 71, 72, 76, 79. **Illustrated by** Emery K. Mitchell

**Cover photograph:** (clockwise from top left) Empanadas de Carne, page 67; Hamburger Steak in the Round, page 3; Pineapple Beans with Meat Balls, page 47; Mushroom-stuffed Meat Loaf, page 36. Photograph by California Beef Council.